HER MAJESTY QUEEN ELIZABETH

The
Queen Mother

THE CELEBRATION OF A LIFE

1900-2002

LINDA A. DOESER
&
KAREN SULLIVAN

This is a Parragon Book
First published in 2002

Parragon
Queen Street House,
4 Queen Street
Bath BA1 1HE, UK

ISBN 0 75259 088 X

Publishing Manager: Sally Harper
Picture Research: Julia Pashley

Produced by Brackenbury Books
Art Director: John Leach
Editorial Director: Linda Doeser
Editors: Eleanor Van Zandt, Leone Edwards

Updated by Foundry Design and Production a part of
The Foundry Creative Media Company Ltd.

Printed in Italy

PICTURE ACKNOWLEDGEMENTS
Camera Press London/Anthony Crickmay: 2; Hulton
Deutsch Collection Limited: frontispiece, 4, 6, 7, 12,
15, 19, 23, 25, 29, 31, 33, 35, 38, 40, 41, 48, 51, 52,
54, 56, 57, 58, 59, 60, 61, 64, 65, 68, 69. 71 top and
centre; Popperfoto: 10,26,34,43,45,63,73; Tim
Graham: 3, 16, 21, 67, 71 bottom, 74,75,76; Topham:
77-83, 85-91; PA Photos: 91,92,93.

Contents

INTRODUCTION
Page 2

LADY ELIZABETH BOWES-LYON
Page 6

DUCHESS OF YORK
Page 24

QUEEN CONSORT
Page 44

QUEEN MOTHER
Page 66

INDEX
Page 94

Introduction

'In Thou, my God, I place my trust without change to the end.'

ONLY THE MOST SENIOR OF CITIZENS can recall a time when HM Queen Elizabeth the Queen Mother was not undertaking a central role in the life of the nation. With her spontaneity, warmth, kindness, graciousness – and what can only be termed majesty – she inspired lasting affection and loyalty at home and abroad, from the time she married the young Duke of York in 1923, through her all too brief reign as Queen Consort and in the long, productive and happy years as Queen Mother. Her death has left an unfillable gap at the very heart of the nation.

Few centuries have been so packed with change, so turbulent and so exciting as the twentieth. The Queen Mother was born just a few months before it began, and for most of it she was at the centre of events. When her quiet, shy husband was forced – so reluctantly and with such little preparation – to become King George VI, few people could have imagined the success he would make of this task. A major part of that success stemmed from the support of his wife. Following his early death in 1952, she created a new role for herself, gaining even greater popularity.

FACING: THE QUEEN MOTHER – AS WE ALL KNEW AND MOST LOVED HER – SMILING SERENELY, STRAIGHT BACKED AND ELEGANTLY TURNED OUT ON HER 90TH BIRTHDAY.

LEFT: A DELIGHTFUL FEMININE FIGURE, THE QUEEN MOTHER CONTRASTS DRAMATICALLY WITH THE SERRIED MILITARY RANKS ON ST. PATRICK'S DAY.

The Queen Mother was undeniably charming, lively and stylish, but there was much more to her. She had courage, strength of character, warm heartedness, integrity and a profound sense of duty. Her religious faith sustained her through times of trouble and informed her entire life. The Strathmore family motto, 'In Thou, my God, I place my trust without change to the end,' was of profound significance to her.

She was a joyous woman, who took pleasure in bringing joy to other people; whether chatting informally to adults and children, robed and regal at state occasions, or elegant and bejewelled at a banquet. She travelled indefatigably across the world – an ambassador of all that is good about Britain. She seemed to take such delight in every task that it was easy to overlook how hard-working she was, yet her schedules, even in her seventies and eighties, were more gruelling than those of almost any other member of the Royal Family. It was typical that she should have remarked, 'Your work is the rent you pay for the room you occupy on earth.'

Informal but never undignified, scrupulous but never boring, highly moral but never censorious, she was tiny in stature but truly majestic in spirit. She was honoured by her husband, the King, and by her daughter, the Queen, and always revered by the peoples of Britain and the Commonwealth.

It was once suggested that she might be appointed Governor-General of Canada, a country with which she had a special rapport. The Queen immediately dismissed the idea: 'Oh, I am afraid not, we could not possibly spare Mummy.' Now that her long life of service has come to an end, there is no choice. The Queen Mother, herself, had no time for mawkish sentimentality and rarely dwelled on or regretted the past, except to recall fond memories. This book follows her example: it is a celebration of her life and a tribute to a Queen.

FACING: THE QUEEN MOTHER – AS MUCH LOVED AS A 'PRIVATE' GRANDMOTHER AS A 'PUBLIC' ONE – CELEBRATES HER 80TH BIRTHDAY WITH HER GRANDCHILDREN. BACK ROW (FROM LEFT TO RIGHT): PRINCE EDWARD, PRINCE CHARLES, PRINCE ANDREW, VISCOUNT LINLEY; FRONT ROW (FROM LEFT TO RIGHT): PRINCESS ANNE, QUEEN ELIZABETH THE QUEEN MOTHER, LADY SARAH ARMSTRONG-JONES.

Lady Elizabeth Bowes-Lyon

'I call myself the Princess Elizabeth.'

THE NINTH CHILD AND FOURTH DAUGHTER of Lord and Lady Glamis – Elizabeth Angela Marguerite – was born, probably at the family home of St. Paul's Walden Bury in Hertfordshire, on Saturday, 4 August 1900. Her father failed to register her birth within 42 days, so she was nearly seven weeks old when, on 21 September, she was entered on the register in Hitchin, Hertfordshire. Lord Glamis had to pay seven shillings and sixpence (37½p) for his delay.

The little girl was born into one of Scotland's most distinguished families. The Lyon family traces its history back to the fourteenth century, when, in 1371, King Robert II of Scotland made Sir John Lyon his Chamberlain. Sir John was given the royal estate of Glamis, the title Thane ('lord') of Glamis and the hand in marriage of the King's daughter Lady Jean Stewart. The family's loyal service to the crown of Scotland in the following turbulent centuries is an impressive record: the then Lord Glamis, together with the King and 12 other earls, was killed fighting at the notorious Battle of Flodden in 1513; the misguided but romantic Mary, Queen of Scots, was a guest of the eighth Lord Glamis; and Bonnie Prince Charlie and 88 companions stayed at Glamis Castle on the way to the bloodbath of Culloden. During this time, further and more senior titles were bestowed, including that of Earl of Strathmore.

In 1767 the ninth Earl of Strathmore married Mary Eleanor Bowes, the daughter and heiress of George Bowes, a wealthy English landowner and Member of Parliament. He agreed to transfer his fortune to the Lyon family on condition that the family name be changed to Bowes by means of a private Act of Parliament. Among the estates that Mary Eleanor inherited was St. Paul's Walden Bury. Her son, the tenth Earl, changed the family name again – this time to Lyon Bowes – and the thirteenth Earl made the final alteration to Bowes-Lyon.

With some testamentary complications, Elizabeth's father, Claude, Lord Glamis, inherited St. Paul's Walden Bury on the death of his grandmother in 1881, together with a considerable acreage of farmland and other property, including two public houses. At the age of 25, he had become a very rich man and felt that he was in a position to propose marriage to Cecilia Cavendish-Bentinck, granddaughter of the Duke of Portland. The Bentinck family, too, had a distinguished history of service to the Crown, dating from the time their Dutch ancestor Hans Bentinck became an adviser – and marriage broker – to William III, Prince of Orange.

The 18-year-old Cecilia and Claude, then an officer in the Life Guards, were married at Petersham parish church on 16 July 1881. Following a honeymoon at Glamis Castle, where the bride was warmly welcomed by the entire clan and the groom, by happy coincidence, did not miss the grouse-shooting season, the newlyweds settled in their home in Hertfordshire. Young as she was, Lady Glamis soon proved to be extremely capable at running the complex household of a late-Victorian aristocrat. Throughout her childhood Elizabeth was to be impressed with the way her mother serenely kept everything operating smoothly, while at the same time welcoming the family's many guests and friends with genuine warmth and hospitality.

ABOVE: DIMINUTIVE AND PRETTY, ELIZABETH COULD EASILY HAVE BECOME TIRESOMELY SPOILT. IN FACT, SHE WAS RENOWNED FOR HER SELF-CONFIDENCE AND SPECIAL KNACK OF PUTTING PEOPLE AT THEIR EASE.

FACING: AN 'AFTERTHOUGHT' HERSELF, ELIZABETH WAS JUST TWO WHEN HER BROTHER DAVID WAS BORN.

The young couple's first child, Violet Hyacinth, was born in April 1882. She was followed by a second daughter, Mary Frances, in August 1883. In September 1884, shortly before her 22nd birthday, Cecilia gave birth to her first son, Patrick. A second son, John Herbert, was born in April 1886, a third, Alexander Francis, in April 1887 and a fourth, Fergus, in April 1889. A third daughter, Rose Constance, was born in May, in 1890. Michael Claude, whom Lord and Lady Glamis thought would be their last child, was born in October 1893. The children split naturally into three groups: the three eldest, Violet, Mary and Patrick; the trio of boys, John, Alexander and Fergus; and, later, the two little ones, Rose and Michael. St. Paul's was expanded to accommodate the growing family and their nannies, tutors and other servants.

Any upper-class British family in the late nineteenth century employed a vast number of servants, including many who worked exclusively in the nurseries and looked after the children. This does not mean that Lady Glamis neglected her children. Far from it; she loved spending time with them and each one learned to read sitting on Mama's lap. The elder ones were sometimes taken to visit neighbours, beginning friendships that were to endure many difficult decades of the next century. Both parents were determined that theirs should be truly a family home – an attitude reflected in their allowing the boys to erect a skittles alley in the former entrance hall.

Life, of course, is never all sunshine and roses. Towards the end of the summer of 1893 the 11-year-old Violet went to stay with her grandmother and aunts in Richmond. Barely a week after giving birth to Michael, on 1 October, Cecilia learned that Violet was ill with diphtheria. She died when her youngest brother was a mere 17 days old, and her funeral was conducted immediately before the baby's christening.

For two such loving parents, this was devastating, but the calls upon their time made by the other children helped them through the immediate period of mourning. They gradually resumed their place in village life and also became involved in a major project to restore the garden and grounds of St. Paul's. A tree-planting programme was undertaken and Cecilia entered into her new hobby with enthusiasm, proving to be an imaginative and talented gardener. The children, too, were encouraged to help. Their parents' response to their renaming the fountain the 'Frying Pan' and christening a classical statue the 'Running Footman' is not recorded.

During term time, at least, life at St. Paul's was relatively quiet with the elder boys away at school and only Rose and Michael still in the nursery. Lady Glamis was fully occupied with her many household responsibilities as well as her numerous other activities. She did beautiful embroidery and was deeply interested in music. Lord Glamis, too, was a busy man with a highly developed sense of responsibility, but he was always glad to return to the family refuge of St. Paul's. As the century came to an end and the year 1900 began, Lady Glamis greeted her husband with the news that she was expecting another baby, seven years after the birth of their last child.

It is said that from the moment Elizabeth opened her startling blue eyes they were smiling. She also inherited her mother's beautiful complexion and delicate features. As she was so much younger than her brothers and sisters, she was destined to be petted and loved and would always occupy a special place in the family. She was not, however, destined to be spoiled and this may have had something to do with the fact that Lord and Lady Glamis finally did complete their family with the birth of a son, David, on 2 May 1902. The two youngest children, nicknamed the 'Benjamins' (after the youngest son of the Biblical patriarch Jacob), became virtually inseparable friends.

Their nursemaid came from the family estate in Whitwell in Hertfordshire. The children found her name, 'Clara', difficult and she became known throughout the family as 'Alah'. She was devoted not just to little Elizabeth, whom she described as 'an exceptionally happy, easy baby', but to the entire Bowes-Lyon family. Apart from presiding over the Benjamins' nursery, she later worked for Elizabeth's sister Mary, who married Lord Elphinstone in 1919, and then became nanny to the Princesses Elizabeth and Margaret Rose. In all, she spent some 45 years with the family.

Less than two years after the birth of their last child, Lord Glamis inherited the earldom. To be precise, he became fourteenth Earl of Strathmore and Kinghorne, Viscount Lyon and Baron Glamis, Tannadyce, Sidlaw and Strathdichtie, Baron Bowes of Streatlam Castle, County Durham and Lunedale, County York – and a very rich man indeed. All the children also acquired titles, the youngest daughter becoming Lady Elizabeth Bowes-Lyon. The family also acquired Glamis Castle and took a lease on No. 20 St. James's Square, in one of the most fashionable parts of London.

St. Paul's remained the family's favourite home and a veritable paradise for the two Benjamins. They had numerous pets – dogs, cats and tortoises, as well as Bobs, a much-beloved Shetland pony. (He used to follow Elizabeth right into the house!) It is hardly surprising that the Queen Mother always remained a countrywoman at heart, considering that so much of her childhood was spent in country pursuits: feeding the chickens, collecting eggs from a building known to the children as the Flea House,

THIS FAMILY PHOTOGRAPH WAS TAKEN IN ABOUT 1904. THE FOUR-YEAR-OLD ELIZABETH IS STANDING BESIDE HER MOTHER. THE OTHER BENJAMIN, TWO-YEAR-OLD DAVID, IS SITTING ON LADY STRATHMORE'S LAP. ELIZABETH'S OTHER BROTHERS AND SISTERS WERE ALMOST A DIFFERENT GENERATION, ALTHOUGH THE FAMILY WAS ALWAYS VERY CLOSE.

where the hens persisted in laying them in preference to the henhouse, roaming through the 'Fairy Wood', playing among the statues and ponds in the garden, and sitting reading beneath the great oak tree with the ring-doves cooing overhead.

Two weeks each year were spent at Streatlam Castle, two months in London at St. James's Square and three months at Glamis. The summer months in Scotland were especially delightful for the children. The entire houschold, including maids, butlers, footmen and, of course, Alah, were packed up for the summer and travel north on the Flying Scotsman to settle at Glamis. Even the beloved pets had to be transported for the long holiday. Glamis was the Earl's favourite place. He loved to entertain on a lavish scale and delighted in the long-standing traditions of his ancient family. When, for example, some 20 or 30 guests were seated for dinner, the Strathmore pipers marched three times around the table, filling the hall with their stirring strains.

It was at Glamis that Elizabeth developed her lifelong interest in fishing; she became renowned for her skill. The shooting season, which so rejoiced her father's heart, was the one dark cloud on her childhood horizon. This less bloodthirsty activity served to divert her attention from the distressing sights and sounds of the guns. Family and servants conspired to keep her away from the annual slaughter and whoever introduced her to this new sport must have been inspired.

There were other pleasures at Glamis. The tennis courts were constantly in use. Indeed, one of Elizabeth's uncles had been a Doubles Champion at Wimbledon and another had been the Scottish champion. Cricket also featured among the activities and Lord Strathmore was known for his straight bat – literally and figuratively.

Indoors, there was a warren of rooms, staircases and attics to explore, hide in and play in. On one occasion, the Benjamins repelled 'raiders' – actually visitors – by pouring buckets of 'boiling oil' over the parapet. Fortunately, the oil in question was only water, but it must have still been something of a shock for the unlucky recipients. The resident ghosts held no fears for Elizabeth, who delighted in

AT A PARTY IN 1909, THE TWO BENJAMINS DANCED A MINUET. MOVED BY THEIR GRAVITY AND GRACE, THE REVEREND JAMES STIRTON, MINISTER OF GLAMIS, ENQUIRED OF THE LITTLE GIRL, 'AND WHO ARE YOU SUPPOSED TO BE, MY DEAR?' WITH NO IDEA OF HOW SIGNIFICANT HER ANSWER WOULD PROVE TO BE, SHE REPLIED, 'I CALL MYSELF THE PRINCESS ELIZABETH'.

recounting spine-chilling stories of the past. Trunks full of dressing-up clothes inspired a family tradition of charades, plays and other games that would later be re-enacted at Buckingham Palace and Windsor Castle by another generation.

It was at Glamis that Elizabeth developed a sense of her own Scottishness. Centuries of noble Scottish blood ran through her veins and the ancient walls of this magnificent castle could not fail to reinforce her awareness of her inheritance. Years later, when visiting South Africa as Queen, she spoke to one of the crowd waiting for her and the King. A Boer, he expressed his admiration and respect for the Queen, and also remarked, 'We still sometimes feel that we can't forgive the English for having conquered us.' Her Lyon ancestry surging to the fore, the Queen replied, 'I understand that perfectly. We feel very much the same in Scotland, too.' It was no coincidence either, that she chose to give birth to her second daughter at Glamis, making Princess Margaret Rose the first member of the Royal Family to be born in Scotland since Prince Robert in 1602. It was to Scotland, too, that she turned for comfort when she bought the Castle of Mey following the death of her husband.

All this was a long way off in those idyllic pre-war years at the beginning of the century and the beginning of her life. Of course, life was not all summer holidays, and the young Elizabeth and her brother had to be educated. Lady Strathmore herself took this in hand to begin with, teaching the children to read and to say their prayers.

Undoubtedly, Lady Strathmore, like most mothers, was more indulgent with her youngest children, but although they could be mischievous, they were never really bad. This had much to do with her own personality – her tranquillity, integrity, sense of fun, kindness and graciousness. One of the older girls later spoke of her mother: 'I never heard her say a harsh word in my life. But we had to obey her, we knew that. We were brought up with very definite principles.' David Bowes-Lyon later described their mother's training. 'My mother taught us to read and write. At the ages of six and seven we could each of us have written a fairly detailed account of all the Bible

stories. This was entirely due to my mother's teaching. She also taught us the rudiments of music, dancing and drawing, at all of which my sister [Elizabeth] became fairly proficient.' Meanwhile, Alah remained the benevolent dictator of the nursery. She was strict but fair, loyal, loving, high-principled, calm and reliable.

A governess was de rigueur for both daughters and young sons at this time, although eventually the dreadful moment would come when David would reach the age of ten and be sent away to school. Of one governess, Elizabeth wrote in her diary, 'Some governesses are nice, some are not'. That, presumably, says it all. When Lady Strathmore engaged Mademoiselle Lang in 1905, she chose one of the 'nice' governesses. Madé, as she became known, was touched by the greeting of the young Elizabeth, who murmured, 'I do hope you will be happy here'. She was happy and remained with the family for some six years.

Thanks to Madé's tutelage, by the age of ten Elizabeth spoke fluent French, but Madé's regime also incorporated many other activities for both study and recreation. She became a loved and trusted friend. It was she who suggested using the schoolroom's best pencil box as a coffin when a cat killed the children's tame bullfinch. On one occasion she accompanied Elizabeth to a garden fête, where her young charge consulted the fortune-teller. Madé asked her what she had been told. Elizabeth replied, 'She was silly. She said I'm going to be a queen when I grow up.'

In 1910 Madé informed Lady Strathmore that she would be leaving the family to marry and return to France. The Benjamins were surprised and upset, but rose to the occasion gracefully and even bought her a special wedding present in addition to the one given by the family. Along with their present, a silver infusion spoon (Madé had once mentioned the difficulty of making good tea in France), they enclosed a card on which they wrote, 'We hope Edmund will be kind to you'.

Kindness was a quality Elizabeth valued and exemplified. Her older sister Rose recalled a stormy night in Glamis Castle, when the Benjamins went to wish their

ELIZABETH INHERITED HER GRACEFULNESS, BEAUTIFUL
EYES AND LOVELY COMPLEXION FROM HER MOTHER,
BUT HER EXTRAORDINARY SELF-POSSESSION WAS
UNIQUELY HER OWN.

THROUGHOUT HER CHILDHOOD, REGULAR CHURCH
ATTENDANCE WAS ROUTINE WHETHER THE FAMILY
WAS AT GLAMIS, LONDON OR ST. PAUL'S – AND THIS
HABIT REMAINED AN ESSENTIAL PART OF ELIZABETH'S
LIFE AS DUCHESS, QUEEN AND QUEEN MOTHER.

mother goodnight. David remembered that he had left a book in the crypt and asked if he might ring for a footman to fetch it. His mother replied that he was quite old enough to fetch it himself and that he was not to ring for anyone. The journey along the dark corridors, past formidable family portraits, suits of armour and an enormous stuffed bear, down to the eerie crypt was a nerve-racking prospect for a boy of eight. Hardly had he set out when he heard his sister's footsteps following behind. With immense kindness and a degree of tact well beyond her years, Elizabeth said, 'Mother said you weren't to ring for someone, but she didn't say you couldn't have me.'

Lady Strathmore related another story characteristic of her youngest daughter. A group of afternoon visitors, unaware that Elizabeth was in the room, were discussing an acquaintance who, although rich, was a rather unattractive young man. Someone said, 'How sad to think that the poor man will be married only for his position and money.' Elizabeth's heart was touched and she instantly betrayed her presence behind the sofa by interpolating, 'Perhaps someone will marry him 'cos she loves him.'

Unquestionably, the strongest influence on the developing child was her mother's. It was through Lady Strathmore that she acquired the unshakable faith that was to see her through many distressing times ahead. Once the Benjamins went to church alone, leaving their mother at home with a cold. They were late and the service had begun, so rather than disturb the congregation, they sat outside and read through the service, saying their prayers and making the responses, before returning home.

The years of family life rolled past, punctuated by a variety of public and private occasions – some happy, some sad. On 21 November 1908, Patrick, Lord Glamis, was married to Lady Dorothy Osborne, daughter of the tenth Duke of Leeds, in the Guards' Chapel at Wellington Barracks. Elizabeth was the youngest of the six bridesmaids and much preoccupied with ensuring that her youngest brother carried out his duties as a trainbearer with proper decorum. The first member of the next generation of the family was born on 1 January 1910, making Elizabeth an aunt. Alah

was transferred to the young Glamis nursery with strict instructions from Elizabeth to report regularly on her nephew's progress. The following year, on 22 June, Earl and Lady Strathmore attended the Coronation of King George V and Queen Mary, while the children watched the procession from a friend's house on the route. That July, Elizabeth became an aunt for the second time when her sister Mary, now Lady Elphinstone, gave birth to a daughter, who was christened Elizabeth Mary.

In the same summer, Alexander fell ill, causing grave anxiety. He seemed to be recovering steadily and the family began to enjoy their usual summer pastimes at Glamis. On 19 October, feeling unwell, he went to bed for the afternoon. To everyone's incredulous grief, he died later that day. It was characteristic that Elizabeth turned her attention to her mother following this tragic loss, gently encouraging her to take up her interests again and to pick up the threads of family life.

In September 1912, David was sent to prep school in Broadstairs, Kent. Elizabeth supervised his packing, hiding small surprises among his clothes, for she knew that he would miss her as much as she would miss him. Lady Strathmore felt that Elizabeth, too, might benefit from the company of companions of her own age and she was enrolled at a small girls' school. She distinguished herself, for Madé had prepared the ground well, and formed a number of friendships, one of them with Elizabeth Cator, who would later become her sister-in-law when she married Michael Bowes-Lyon.

However, formal schooling was not really to Elizabeth's taste, and she welcomed a new governess in April 1913. Breaking with the tradition of employing a French or British governess, Lady Strathmore employed a young German woman, Kathie Kuebler, who approached her duties with characteristic Teutonic thoroughness. Piano lessons came before breakfast, conversation was always in German and everything, from nature study to geography, from needlework to gymnastics, ran to a strictly observed timetable. Fräulein Kuebler found Elizabeth a 'gifted and willing pupil' and the two formed a close and lasting friendship.

LADY STRATHMORE WAS AN AFFECTIONATE WOMAN AND A DEEPLY LOVING PARENT. SHE FORMED EXCEPTIONALLY CLOSE TIES WITH HER YOUNGEST DAUGHTER DURING THE BLEAK AND STRESSFUL YEARS OF WORLD WAR I.

When David returned for the holidays that year, more family anxiety followed as he developed appendicitis. The family awaited the outcome of surgery with trepidation. Fortunately, Fräulein Kuebler was able to help her young pupil through this trying time. Her own brother of much the same age had undergone an appendectomy only four weeks earlier. A letter from Germany announcing his complete recovery provided at least some comfort to the distraught Elizabeth.

Happily, David did recover, and the two Benjamins spent a delightful holiday visiting exhibitions, theatres and even the recently opened New Gallery Cinema. Among their activities was a junior dance given by family friends. Fräulein, of course, chaperoned the young people. She noted that Elizabeth 'met the children of the King' and danced with Prince Albert. (Albert or 'Bertie' was the name by which King George VI was known throughout his childhood and youth.)

Once she reached the age of 13, Elizabeth was 'promoted' to a more grown-up position in the household. She was allowed to join the luncheon table even when there were guests. There she met many eminent statesmen, politicians, ambassadors and other distinguished figures – a rare privilege for one so young.

In June 1914 the Hapsburg Archduke Ferdinand was assassinated in Sarajevo. Rumours of war abounded, and Fräulein Kuebler, who had already agreed to remain with the Strathmores for a further four years, left for her summer holidays with great anxiety. On bidding her good-bye, Lady Strathmore begged her to return.

As a birthday treat on 4 August 1914, Elizabeth was taken to the Coliseum, a London theatre, to see a programme of sketches, singers and the Russian ballerina Federovna. Earlier in the day the Prime Minister had told Parliament that Britain had issued an ultimatum to Germany: if German troops were not withdrawn from Belgium by midnight, Britain would have to declare war. The streets were packed with crowds waving flags and chattering excitedly as Elizabeth and her family drove to the theatre. When they awoke the next morning the country was at war .

Within days Patrick was called up to the officers' reserve of the Black Watch, John and Fergus joined the Black Watch, although they were in different regiments, and Michael enlisted in the Royal Scots. Both John and Fergus immediately proposed marriage to the young ladies of their choice. Rose went to London to train as a nurse, and the 60-year-old Earl resumed his uniform. Elizabeth and Lady Strathmore went to Glamis to transform it into a reception centre and hospital. Life there was marked, as the Queen Mother later recalled, by 'the bustle of hurried visits to chemists for outfits of every sort of medicine, and to gunsmiths to buy all the things that people thought they wanted for a war and found they didn't'. Elizabeth ran endless errands under her mother's supervision. Public opinion was that it would all be over by Christmas.

The first casualties arrived at Glamis in December 1914. By 1919, when the last men left, more than 1,500 officers and men had spent time there convalescing and recovering from the 'war to end all wars'. When Rose had completed her training she returned to Glamis to work. The Red Cross played a key role and the village provided volunteers. In planning the conversion of the Castle, Lady Strathmore had decided that there should be minimal reorganization in order to provide a warm and welcoming atmosphere. Lady Strathmore greeted each man as he arrived and made sure that he had adequate tobacco or cigarettes. Quite clearly, some rooms, including the huge dining room, needed to be turned into hospital wards and were filled with rows of beds, and the crypt was turned into a mess room. Family treasures were moved upstairs out of harm's way – Elizabeth had been delegated to supervise this – but otherwise the Castle was kept, as far as possible, as it was in peace time.

Elizabeth was responsible for collecting mail and helping the men keep in touch with their families, as well as running many errands on their behalf. Lady Asquith tells of a soldier whose arm had been wounded and whose parents were afraid that it would have to be amputated. He sent them a photograph, but, unfortunately, the injured arm was concealed and they thought that their fears had been realized. When

FACING: REMEMBRANCE DAY WAS ALWAYS ESPECIALLY POIGNANT FOR THE QUEEN MOTHER, WHOSE PERSONAL MEMORIES ENCOMPASSED BOTH WORLD WARS. SHE IS SEEN HERE WITH THE PRINCESS OF WALES AND KING OLAF OF NORWAY.

a family friend informed the soldier of his parents' distress, he consulted Elizabeth. Characteristically, she took immediate action, sending them another photograph with the arm clearly in view and a reassuring letter about their son's progress. In later years, many men recalled her special acts of kindness and thoughtfulness.

It was not, of course, all over by Christmas, but Lady Strathmore and Elizabeth were determined that the holiday should still be a festive occasion. A Christmas tree was installed and Red Cross parcels were wrapped as gifts. However, Elizabeth noticed that not many parcels were arriving for the men, so at the last minute she raided the village shop for small items, such as playing cards, pens and pencils, so that each convalescent had a personal present from her.

The year 1915 brought a change in the nature of the war and in the nature of the visitors to Glamis Castle. The first patients had been truly convalescent – destined, in fact, to return to the trenches of Flanders and France. The men arriving in 1915 were exchanged prisoners of war, many permanently maimed and disfigured and some desperately scarred psychologically. Elizabeth must have been profoundly affected by these terrible injuries, but she maintained her cheerful helpfulness and good nature.

In September Fergus visited the Castle on few hours' leave. He left Glamis on the 22nd. The Battle of Loos started on Thursday, 25 September, and Fergus was killed in the taking of the Hohenzollern Redoubt. All the patients signed a letter of sympathy to the family and, as a mark of respect, refrained from playing the piano, making any noise in the grounds and using the rooms nearest to the family quarters. Lady Strathmore was touched by their thoughtfulness, but sent a message to say that 'her guests' should resume their normal activities. However, Elizabeth now took her mother's place to greet new arrivals and say good-bye to those who were leaving.

A happy family occasion occurred on 24 May 1916. Rose was married to Commander William Spencer Leveson Gower at St. James's, Piccadilly, and Elizabeth was one of the three bridesmaids. After the wedding, Lady Strathmore and Elizabeth returned to Glamis Castle. There, in her sister's absence and with her mother's continuing grief for Fergus and anxiety for her other sons, Elizabeth took on increased responsibility. She also made every effort gently to encourage her mother to pick up the threads again as she had in the months following Alexander's death. Gradually, Lady Strathmore began to resume her normal duties, finding solace in her faith. Every morning, she and Elizabeth went to the Castle chapel for private prayers. When some of the soldiers learned of this, they asked if they, too, might share in the prayers.

In 1917 the War Office notified the Strathmores that Michael had been killed in action. Hoping that David would comfort their parents, the sisters arranged for him to come home from Eton. He arrived, but refused to wear a black tie, insisting that Michael was not dead. There is a tradition of second sight in the Lyon family and David claimed to have seen his brother with a bandaged head in a large house surrounded by fir trees. Some three months later, the family learned that Michael had been shot through the head and was a prisoner of war.

In November 1918 the guns on the Western Front fell silent. The last patients did not leave Glamis, however, until late in 1919. Characteristically, Elizabeth threw her energies into helping them with demobilization and finding jobs and homes.

Gradually life returned to normal, although it would never be the same for anyone. St. Paul's Walden Bury was reopened, Michael returned home and there was a crop of post-war weddings. However, the years that Elizabeth could normally have expected to spend at balls and parties, enjoying all the pleasures of a gradually maturing young woman on the brink of adulthood, had been spent very differently. She had been thrust, without choice, into maturity and responsibility, but had accepted her duties willingly and graciously – as she would in the years to come.

ELIZABETH WAS 18 BY THE TIME THE ARMISTICE CAME. THE TRADITION OF PRESENTING DEBUTANTES AT COURT HAD BEEN SUSPENDED FOR THE DURATION. WHEN IT WAS REINSTATED, SHE CEDED PRECEDENCE TO HER SENIOR SISTER-IN-LAW. BY THE TIME HER OWN TURN WOULD HAVE COME ROUND, SHE WAS ALREADY A MEMBER OF THE ROYAL FAMILY.

Duchess of York

'You will be a lucky fellow if she accepts you.'

COCKTAILS AND FLAPPERS, the Charleston and chain-smoking – the Roaring Twenties; not really an environment that Lord and Lady Strathmore, or Elizabeth herself, regarded as being congenial. Always light-hearted – even in her nineties – but never mindlessly frivolous, Elizabeth entered this lively decade determined to enjoy herself, but with maturity beyond her years.

She was stunningly lovely, vital and radiant, with beautiful skin, a trim and feminine figure, sparkling blue eyes and a natural warmth, serenity and charm. She was a witty conversationalist and a splendid dancer. Small wonder, then, that she had many friends and admirers and that she turned not a few heads.

Among her friends was Princess Mary, only daughter of King George V and Queen Mary. The Princess was three years older than Elizabeth and they had met briefly on a number of occasions. During the war Elizabeth had become involved in fund-raising activities, among her many other voluntary commitments. When Princess Mary inspected the Forfarshire Girl Guides, she was formally introduced to Elizabeth and

BERTIE, OR PRINCE ALBERT AS HE SHOULD MORE PROPERLY BE CALLED, WAS NOT A MAN OF IMMENSE INTELLECT. NEVERTHELESS, HE KNEW WHAT HE WANTED – ELIZABETH BOWES-LYON – AND PURSUED HER WITH SINGLE-MINDED DETERMINATION.

ELIZABETH HAD ENDURED A PERIOD OF PAINFUL
INDECISION BEFORE SHE ACCEPTED BERTIE'S FINAL
PROPOSAL OF MARRIAGE ON A WALK ONE WEEKEND
AT ST. PAUL'S IN JANUARY 1923.

this launched their friendship. Lady Airlie, the Strathmores' neighbour and Lady-in-Waiting and confidante to Queen Mary, fostered this friendship and soon encouraged a closer relationship between the Princess's brother Bertie and Lady Elizabeth.

A romantic story links the love between these two to a childhood incident. Apparently, the five-year-old Lady Elizabeth attended a birthday party, given by Lady Leicester, at which Bertie was also a guest. Although about five years older than her, he was shy with little self-confidence. Feeling sorry for the stammering and awkward Prince, Elizabeth picked the cherries from the top of her cake and gave them to him. When they met again, more than a dozen years later, he is said to have recognized her and instantly fallen in love. It is probably not true – but it should be!

Throughout her life, the Queen Mother preserved her privacy, while remaining enormously popular with the public. In later years the Clarence House staff jealously guarded details of her personal life in a way that few other Royal Households have managed in these days of paparazzi and ruthless tabloid newspapers. Her secret, perhaps, was that she made herself totally and enthusiastically available as a public figure – Duchess, Consort and Queen Mother – and so the same public felt that she was justified in remaining private as wife, mother and widow. Whatever the reason, details of the time that Prince Bertie and Lady Elizabeth first met as adults have never been clarified. What is known is that they probably encountered each other during 1919 when Elizabeth was Princess Mary's occasional guest at Buckingham Palace.

Certainly they danced together at Lord and Lady Farquhar's house in Grosvenor Square in 1920. At the age of 25, Bertie was still painfully shy and many people had remarked on how unwilling he had been to take a partner at a naval dance shortly before this. Nevertheless, he waltzed with Elizabeth, and clearly enjoyed the occasion.

The Prince's life had been very different from that of his future wife. He started out badly by being born on the anniversary of Prince Albert's death, which, even 44 years later, was still regarded as a day of mourning by Queen Victoria. His being named Albert in memory of his great grandfather did little to endear him to the Queen, of whom he was rather frightened. Bertie was the second son, although by the time his father, King George V, came to the throne, three more sons and a daughter had been born. Bertie had inherited his mother's shyness and this was probably aggravated by his being forced to use his right hand against his natural inclination towards left-handedness. That may also have been the cause of the stammer which plagued him for much of his life. King George V treated his family as if he were commanding a battleship, and what he thought of as good-natured teasing was painfully abrasive to his sensitive second son. His mother was little comfort in the difficult relationship with his father, for, although she genuinely loved her children, she had a very highly developed sense of duty, which once led her to say, 'I must always remember that their father is also their King.'

Bertie was persistent, however, and, although never brilliant intellectually, he worked hard at Dartmouth Naval College and acquitted himself honourably on active service in the Great War. Shortly before the dance at the Farquhars', the King bestowed upon him the title Duke of York, a title the King had borne himself and a singular honour which the Prince fully appreciated.

Bertie may have fallen in love instantly with Elizabeth, but her heart was free and there was no thought of marriage on her mind. After the disruptive years of the war and the family losses and separations she was keen to remain a little longer with her beloved parents and her brothers and sisters. However, one change did take place in 1920 when the lease of 20 St. James's Square expired. After some searching, Lady Strathmore settled on a new London house, 17 Bruton Street.

While the new house was being redecorated and generally prepared for the Strathmores, the family followed its usual pattern travelling to Glamis for the summer. Lady Airlie was entertaining Princess Mary and the Duke of York at her Scottish home, Cortachy Castle. Lord Strathmore invited the party to visit Glamis and

this began a succession of visits, ostensibly for the shooting. The Duke was also made welcome at St. Paul's on a number of occasions. Welcome is undoubtedly what he felt. The informal family atmosphere, the exuberant sense of fun, the warmth and affection that permeated the household and, most of all, the presence of Elizabeth must have enchanted him. He began to lose a little of his shyness, and, at the same time, his affections became fixed. Elizabeth certainly liked the Prince, but she had many admirers and, perhaps more importantly, she was extremely doubtful about undertaking the responsibilities of becoming the King's daughter-in-law.

In spring 1921 Bertie spoke to his parents about his desire to ask Lady Elizabeth Bowes-Lyon to marry him. The Queen had already enquired about her from Lady Airlie, whose response had been that she could say nothing but good of her. The King sent a note to his son which said, 'You will be a lucky fellow if she accepts you.' She did not accept him. Lady Strathmore was too loving a mother to try to persuade her daughter into a marriage against her inclinations and too much of an aristocrat to be dazzled by the prospect of a royal connection. Nevertheless, she felt very sorry for the rebuffed Prince and assured him of a continuing welcome at St. Paul's and Glamis.

One person who had been especially disappointed was Lady Airlie, so she was particularly delighted when, that same summer, the Queen, who was staying at Cortachy Castle, together with the Duke of York and Princess Mary, expressed a desire to visit Glamis. Lady Strathmore was unwell and Elizabeth had taken on the responsibilities of running the household and of acting as hostess to the many guests who came for the shooting. She acted as hostess, too, to the royal visitors, and her impeccable manners and natural charm impressed Queen Mary – no small feat.

The engagement of Elizabeth's friend Princess Mary to Lord Lascelles was announced in November 1921, and the wedding took place in Westminster Abbey on 28 February 1922. The bridesmaids were Lady Mary Cambridge, Lady May Cambridge, Lady Mary Thynne, Diamond Hardinge and Lady Elizabeth Bowes-Lyon.

IT IS MUCH TO ELIZABETH'S CREDIT THAT SHE
SUCCESSFULLY CAPTURED NOT ONLY THE RESPECT BUT
THE GENUINE AFFECTION OF THE KING AND QUEEN,
WHO WERE EQUALLY RENOWNED FOR THEIR
EXCEPTIONAL STANDARDS OF BEHAVIOUR AND THEIR
UNEMOTIONAL PERSONALITIES. IN PARTICULAR, SHE
ESTABLISHED AN IMMEDIATE RAPPORT WITH THE
INTROVERTED QUEEN AND THE TWO BECAME
STAUNCH ALLIES THROUGHOUT THE MANY
TROUBLESOME AND STORM-TOSSED YEARS AHEAD.

A little over a year later, four of them would once again be bridesmaids at the wedding of the fifth.

The Duke and Elizabeth began to meet more often. His feelings for her deepened and were increasingly apparent to friends and family. In fact, it is likely that some of his friends conspired to bring the two together at their dinner and theatre parties. Meanwhile, Elizabeth was becoming aware that her feelings for the Duke were stronger than mere liking and friendship, but she remained very uncertain about the weight of duty, the lack of privacy and the strain on family life that such a marriage implied. She was also very aware of the strength of the Duke's feelings. It is an interesting footnote that she declined five other proposals of marriage – all from extremely eligible men – at this time.

In the winter of 1923 the Duke visited the Strathmores at St. Paul's. On Saturday, 13 January, he and Elizabeth went for stroll in the woods, where he proposed again. This time she accepted. The Duke immediately sent a telegram to his parents which said, 'All right, Bertie.' The following day he dashed off to Sandringham full of his news. The Queen expressed her delight, acknowledging the happiness that shone from her second son. The King, too, was pleased and wrote in his diary, 'Bertie … informed us that he was engaged to Elizabeth Bowes-Lyon, to which we gladly gave our consent. I trust they will be very happy.' That trust was to be fulfilled.

A few days later Elizabeth described herself as happy but dazed and as the crescendo built up towards the wedding, life became something of a whirl. The engagement was announced in the Court Circular on Tuesday, 16 January, and Lady Elizabeth Bowes-Lyon became a name on everyone's lips. With charming naïveté, Elizabeth gave a spontaneous personal interview to Mr. Cozens-Hardy, a reporter from The Star, an event not repeated by any member or about-to-be member of the Royal Family since. On 20 January, Lord and Lady Strathmore, together with Elizabeth, paid a formal visit to the King and Queen at Sandringham. Sacks of telegrams, letters, gifts and good wishes poured into Bruton Street. The wedding was planned to take place on Thursday, 26 April 1923 in Westminster Abbey.

Characteristically, Elizabeth chose to have her wedding dress made of Nottingham lace. This not only provided work for those in the deeply depressed lace trade but also served as an advertisement for British textiles. She had quite a hand in the design, which was made by Handley-Seymour, and was also responsible for the employment of a local seamstress to work on the trousseau and bridesmaids' dresses. Her engagement ring, which the Duke insisted she should choose herself, was a large Kashmir sapphire set between two diamonds.

As the crowds began to gather on the eve of the wedding, the rain started to fall. It stopped at 9.30 in the morning. At 11.08 the King and Queen set off. At precisely

NO KING'S SON HAD BEEN MARRIED AT WESTMINSTER ABBEY FOR MORE THAN 500 YEARS. MOREOVER, THIS CHARMING, SMILING BRIDE WAS A SCOTTISH GIRL OF GOOD FAMILY — NOT A FOREIGN PRINCESS — AND THE PEOPLE OF BRITAIN TOOK HER TO THEIR HEARTS THAT OVERCAST DAY IN 1923 AND HELD ON TO HER FOR MORE THAN SEVEN DECADES.

FACING: THE FORMAL WEDDING PHOTOGRAPHS WERE MORE RESTRAINED BUT NOT REALLY VERY DIFFERENT FROM THOSE TAKEN AT ROYAL WEDDINGS TODAY. LEFT TO RIGHT (STANDING): LADY MARY CAMBRIDGE, DUCHESS OF YORK, DUKE OF YORK, LADY MAY CAMBRIDGE. LEFT TO RIGHT (MIDDLE ROW): DIAMOND HARDINGE, LADY MARY THYNNE, LADY KATHARINE HAMILTON, BETTY CATOR. LEFT TO RIGHT (FRONT ROW): ELIZABETH ELPHINSTONE, CECILIA BOWES-LYON.

11.12 Elizabeth left Bruton Street. Exactly one minute later, the Duke, the Prince of Wales, his chief supporter (the royal equivalent of 'best man'), and Prince Henry, left the Palace. He wore the uniform of a Royal Air Force Group Captain, with the Riband and Star of the Order of the Garter and the Star of the Order of the Thistle, recently awarded by the King as a tribute to his future daughter-in-law.

Elizabeth rode in a landau, but, because she was still a commoner she was accompanied by four mounted policeman rather than a Royal Guard of Honour. She drew up at the Abbey at 11.30 and stepped down to the cheers of the crowds to be joined by her father; two trainbearers, her nieces Elizabeth Elphinstone, Mary's daughter, and Cecilia Bowes-Lyon, Patrick's daughter; and six bridesmaids. They were Lady Mary Cambridge, Lady May Cambridge, Lady Mary Thynne, Lady Elizabeth Cator, Lady Katherine Hamilton and Diamond Hardinge.

George V maintained afterwards that the sun came out at precisely the moment the bride entered the Abbey. As she did so, she turned aside to lay her bouquet of York roses and Scottish heather on the Tomb of the Unknown Soldier before proceeding to the altar. With this spontaneous and touching gesture, she established a tradition that all royal brides have followed since, except that they have left their bouquets after the wedding and not gone to the altar flowerless. The Archbishop of Canterbury read the wedding service and the Archbishop of York addressed the bride and groom.

After the ceremony the Duke and Duchess of York left the Abbey and rode in the Glass Coach – extremely slowly and via a long detour – through the crowds back to the Palace, pausing briefly at the Cenotaph on the way. At Buckingham Palace a sumptuous wedding breakfast of eight courses awaited, but first the Royal Family – and especially its new member – had to make the traditional appearance on the famous balcony. They did so to a sea of waving handkerchiefs and a roar of cheering good wishes. It was a cold day, and Queen Mary thoughtfully wrapped a shawl around her new daughter-in-law's shoulders.

IN A HAIL OF CONFETTI AND ROSE PETALS, THE
NEWLYWEDS LEFT THE PALACE – AND THEIR 123
GUESTS – IN A LANDAU DRAWN BY FOUR GREY HORSES
ON THE FIRST STAGE OF THEIR HONEYMOON.

Less than two hours later, dressed in a long-waisted, mushroom-coloured dress and wearing a feathered hat, the fourth lady in the land left in an open landau for her honeymoon. The carriage was drawn by four grey horses and they were bombarded with confetti and rose petals all the way to Waterloo station, where the Prince of Wales saw the couple aboard their flower-lined carriage. The entire route of the brief journey to Bookham, Surrey, was lined with cheering crowds. For the first few days of their honeymoon, the Duke and Duchess stayed at Polesden Lacey, the Regency house of Mrs. Ronald Greville. It was here, at a press photographers' session on the third day of their marriage, that it was announced that Elizabeth would be accorded the title 'Her Royal Highness'. Now, 14 years after her performance as a make-believe princess at Glamis, she would truly be Princess Elizabeth. On 9 May, the newlyweds arrived at Glamis. The weather in Scotland was unseasonably cold and miserable and the Duchess developed whooping cough, a most unromantic beginning.

The couple then stayed briefly at Frogmore House, part of the Windsor estate, before moving, on 7 June, to their new home, White Lodge in Richmond Park. This 200-year-old hunting lodge had been given to Queen Mary by her parents, the Duke and Duchess of Teck, in 1869. It was mark of great favour that the Queen granted the Lodge to her son and his new wife, but, perhaps like many blessings in life, this one was mixed. The furnishings were very formal – in some cases dismal – although the bride was well provided with wedding presents that did much to brighten her new home. A greater problem was the lack of privacy. Neither the Duke nor the Duchess could venture out of doors without being besieged by hordes of well-meaning but intrusive sightseers. Later in the year a further difficulty was discovered. Sudden and impenetrable fogs were prone to descend upon the park, and on more than one occasion the Yorks' chauffeur completely lost all sense of direction.

Royal life now began in earnest. The attractive and engaging Duchess was greatly in demand for visits and patronage. She acquired her first presidency – that of the

Scottish Women's Hospital Association – almost immediately. Shortly after the couple moved to Richmond, Princess Christian, Queen Victoria's third daughter, died and the newest member of the Royal Family inherited her charitable interests. She entertained a group of Dr. Barnado's girls who were emigrating. One said later that she treated them 'as if we were real friends'. An observer who had watched her lay a foundation stone commented, 'I suppose Her Royal Highness has laid many foundation stones, yet she seems this afternoon to be discovering a new and delightful occupation.'

She never lost this remarkable ability to make an event that was special in the lives of the people who had invited her seem special to her, too. From the very beginning, she successfully combined the royal and the common touch. She was always genuinely interested in meeting people and really listened to what they had to say to her. She was profoundly conscious of the responsibility that her privileged position carried and she simply liked to bring joy to other people.

Besides taking on a gruelling round of official duties – sometimes she had as many as eight engagements in a single day – the new Duchess had also to learn the pattern of life at Court. The King had very traditional ideas and little had changed since the days when his grandmother had occupied the throne. When there were dinner guests, the ladies always executed a full curtsy to the King before leaving the gentlemen to their port. If the Duchess had one failing that she never learned to cure, it was unpunctuality. It is a measure of the King's affection that his response to her apology for being late for dinner – in anyone else, an unforgivable offence – was, 'You are not late my dear, I think we must have sat down two minutes too early.' On another occasion, when someone complained of her perennial lateness, he replied, 'Ah, but if she weren't late, she would be perfect, and how horrible that would be.'

The most important of the Duchess's new roles was to provide support and strength to her husband. She encouraged his special interest in the Industrial Welfare Society and the running of Boys' Camps. She provided the first real home that he had

NEVER ONE TO DO THINGS BY HALVES, THE NEW DUCHESS TRIED HER HAND AT THE COCONUT SHY AT THE FRESH AIR FUND OUTING AT LOUGHTON. INSTANT PUBLIC ACCESS AND A DELIGHTFUL SENSE OF FUN WERE TWO OF THE DUCHESS'S MOST ENDEARING AND ENDURING CHARACTERISTICS.

had, filling the draughty rooms and corridors of White Lodge with the warmth of her love. She also persuaded him to see an expatriate Australian speech therapist, Lionel Logue. Not only did the Duke's slight stammer make public speaking extremely difficult, but it caused him excruciating embarrassment. Mr. Logue devised a series of breathing exercises, having succeeded in convincing the Duke that his problem stemmed from his diaphragm, not from his speech, let alone his intellect. The Duchess was responsible for seeing that these exercises were carried out, a duty she fulfilled faithfully. In less than a month the improvement in the Duke's speech was noticeable and the boost this gave to his confidence was immeasurable. He never lost his dislike of speaking in public – but he certainly lost his terror of it.

The King was anxious not to overdo the demands on the 'little Duchess', although the formidable list of official engagements she undertook in the first year of her marriage makes one wonder what his idea of 'overdoing' could have been. Certainly he vetoed any suggestion of a major tour in what were then called the Dominions. However, for reasons of diplomacy, the Foreign Office was keen that the Duke and Duchess should accept an invitation to the country then known as the Kingdom of the Serbs, Croats and Slovenes to celebrate the baptism of Peter, the heir to the throne, and also to represent King George V at Prince's Paul's wedding to Princess Olga of Greece. (Prince Paul was the baby Crown Prince's cousin and later acted as Regent.) The Duke and Duchess duly acted as godparents to the baby Prince. They had to assume their responsibilities rather early, when the baby was accidentally dropped into the font by the Patriarch and was then rescued from drowning by his quick-thinking godfather. At the wedding, the following day, 22 October 1923, the Duchess had an opportunity to meet many members of the family. All of them were charmed by her, especially Queen Marie of Romania.

On returning to England the Yorks were caught up in many official and social activities – from Christmas visits to disabled children to two royal weddings, from visiting factories to attending a state ball. Meanwhile, they took temporary refuge in Princess Mary's London house, as the White Lodge was becoming increasingly difficult to run. On 19 July 1924 the Duke and Duchess were sent on an official visit to Northern Ireland, where, again, they were greeted with real affection. The Duke continued to be impressed with the way his wife seemed completely at ease and full of good humour without once losing her dignity. That she was so successful on such occasions was immensely helpful to him; his confidence grew and his public manner became more relaxed. The Duchess had slipped easily into the royal role that she would occupy in different ways for most of the century, although at that time she had no knowledge of the responsibilities that her family would be called upon to shoulder.

In the summer of 1924 she informed her mother that she was expecting a child. Following the Christmas holiday at Sandringham, the Duchess accepted her mother's suggestion that she should stay at Bruton Street. Apart from other reasons, she was worried that if she gave birth at White Lodge, medical assistance might get lost on its way to her! It was also arranged that Alah should now transfer to the Duchess's household to look after the new baby.

Ever since the incident of the alleged 'warming pan baby' during the reign of James II, when some Protestants claimed that a live, non-royal boy had been substituted, concealed in a warming pan, for a dead prince born to James and his Catholic wife Mary of Modena, it has been the custom for the Home Secretary to attend all births of royal children in line of succession. On 20 April 1926, both the Duchess's doctors and Sir William Joynson-Hicks, Home Secretary, were called to Bruton Street. It was a false alarm. However, during the night Sir William was called out of his bed by the obstetric consultant Sir Henry Simpson, who informed him that 'a certain line of treatment [had] been decided upon'. This was probably a Caesarean operation, although the facts have never been made known. The Queen Mother always regarded details of the birth as being her private concern and not for public consumption. How

No one, least of all her parents, had any idea that the delightful little girl that the young Duke and Duchess welcomed with such pride and excitement in 1926 would have to undertake the tremendous responsibilities of monarchy while still only 25 years old.

she felt about having the event witnessed by the Home Secretary can be imagined.

The King and Queen were awakened at 4 o'clock in the morning to be informed that 'darling Elizabeth' had given birth to a girl at 2.40 a.m. The Duke and Duchess were thrilled with their daughter and asked permission to call her Elizabeth Alexandra Mary, a graceful tribute to the King's mother and to the Queen, and she was duly so-christened in the private chapel of Buckingham Palace on 29 May. Princess Mary was one of her six godparents. Although at this time the Princess was third in line to the throne, it was likely that the Yorks would have a boy, who would take precedence, and, in any case, everyone expected that the Prince of Wales would marry.

In 1926 the Prime Minister of Australia asked the King if he would send one of his elder sons to represent him at the official opening of the new Federal Parliament in Canberra. This was project dear to the King's heart and he knew that the Duke and Duchess of York were keen to play a role in cementing relations between Britain and the Dominions. He was concerned, however, that such a responsibility might prove too great for his son's confidence. Despite these misgivings, he suggested that the Duke should represent him, but the Prime Minister was, apparently, 'appalled' by the idea. None of this did anything to help the Duke's new-found but somewhat shaky self-confidence. The Duchess had no such doubts. It was she who persuaded the King and Queen that refusing the Duke would do him irreparable harm and that he was fully capable of undertaking all the duties required – including speaking in public.

Neither the Australians nor the New Zealanders were enthusiastic when they heard that the Duke and Duchess were to visit. They had hoped for a return of the glamorous Prince of Wales. The Duchess's only reservation about the trip concerned leaving Princess Elizabeth – although she would undoubtedly be lovingly cared for by the devoted Alah and both sets of grandparents.

From the moment they landed in New Zealand, the Duchess stole the hearts of the waiting crowds. Her expression of lively interest never faltered throughout the

ABOVE: NO ONE COULD ACCUSE THE DUCHESS OF BEING 'STUFFY' – AND THE CHANCE OF CATCHING SOME WILY TROUT WHILE VISITING NEW ZEALAND WAS TOO GOOD TO MISS.

FACING: THE DUKE'S SENSE OF RESPONSIBILITY AND THE DUCHESS'S EXUBERANT CHARM WON GENUINE AFFECTION THROUGHOUT AUSTRALIA AND, INCIDENTALLY, GENUINE RESPECT FROM THE KING AND QUEEN.

exhausting tour. The Duke made his speeches with great aplomb, but it was the Duchess who made a greater impact even than the Prince of Wales had done. It was typical that she recognized among all the crowds a former soldier whom she had nursed at Glamis during the war, and that she should call him over to talk to her.

Early in the visit, the Duchess developed tonsillitis, and the Duke wanted to cancel the rest of the tour, convinced that it was wife that the crowds were really waiting to see. She persuaded him to continue and he acquitted himself well. She was recovered in time to support and encourage her husband when they continued their trip to Australia. They won the affections of everybody they met – the Duchess with her charm and the Duke with his purposeful sense of responsibility. It was said afterwards that Australia was the 'making of the Yorks'.

Back in England, reunited with their daughter, they were surprised and touched to find a crowd calling for them outside Buckingham Palace. The King and Queen were struck with the demeanour of their son. Probably for the first time in his life, they compared him favourably with the Prince of Wales whose glamorous image and easy manner had overshadowed his less confident younger brother for many years. That was the Duchess's doing.

In 1924 the Yorks moved to 145 Piccadilly, which remained their home for nine and a half years. The Duchess planned to concentrate on establishing a peaceful and private family life, insofar as royal duties permitted this. Her approach to motherhood was based on Lady Strathmore's, and Princess Elizabeth saw as much of her parents as possible, taking an increasing part in the family's social life as she grew older.

At the beginning of 1930, the Duchess informed her family that she was expecting another child. With the growing worry about the unwillingness of the Prince of Wales to 'settle down', there was considerable hope within the Royal Family that she would produce a 'boy of York'. Whatever the sex, this second child, the Duchess insisted, would be born at Glamis Castle. A series of false alarms for nearly two weeks in

August 1930 caused the Home Secretary (who seemed genuinely to believe that a royal birth in Scotland might well presage something doubtful) to come close to a nervous breakdown. However, he was at the Castle, with half an hour to spare, on 21 August, when the Duchess gave birth to a second daughter.

The Yorks wanted to call the new Princess Anne Margaret, but the King disliked the name Anne, so they eventually settled on Margaret Rose. There was not to be a 'boy of York', but the King's two granddaughters brought him immeasurable joy in the last years of his life.

The round of royal duties continued against a background of increasing concern over the King's health and the fecklessness of the Prince of Wales. The Duke and Duchess of York were granted a country home, Royal Lodge in Windsor Great Park, in September 1931, and this provided the same kind of family haven as St. Paul's had throughout the Duchess's childhood. One observer said of them at this time, 'I can honestly say that never in my whole life have I seen a family so happy.' Weekends were spent at Windsor and weekdays – now involving Miss Crawford, the children's much-loved governess 'Crawfie' – were spent at 145 Piccadilly. A newspaper in the 1930s referred to this house as 'the home at the heart of the Empire' – and always at the heart of the home was the Duchess.

In May 1935 King George V celebrated his Silver Jubilee – the 25th anniversary of his accession to the throne. The gruff old King was surprised and touched by the enthusiasm of the waiting crowds who cheered him and the Queen throughout the week's celebrations. Appropriately, the Duke and Duchess of York represented the King at the Jubilee festivities held in Edinburgh.

The joy was to be short-lived. In June, the King collapsed and was ordered by his doctors to rest. The death of his only sister in December was a setback to the 70-year-old King's recovery and Christmas at Sandringham lacked its usual sparkle. The Duchess of York also fell ill at Christmas with influenza, which then turned to

pneumonia. She insisted that her husband should travel to Norfolk to see his father and to support his mother. When the Duke returned he told her that the King was seriously ill and might not recover. On 19 January, it was clear that he was dying, and his sons and members of the Privy Council attended him in his last hours at Sandringham. He died just before midnight on 20 January.

The Duchess of York travelled immediately to offer what comfort she could to Queen Mary. During the 12 years of her marriage, the Duchess had formed a close bond with her mother-in-law, and both she and the Duke were an immense support to the bereaved Queen.

After all the ceremonial attendant on the death of a King – the lying in state and the funeral procession through the streets of London – Queen Mary let it be known that she wished still to be called 'Queen Mary' and not 'the Queen Mother'. It was left to her daughter-in-law some 17 years later to make that title supremely her own.

THE DUKE AND DUCHESS, TOGETHER WITH PRINCESS MARGARET AND AN INQUISITIVE PRINCESS ELIZABETH, ARRIVE AT ST. PAUL'S CATHEDRAL FOR THE THANKSGIVING SERVICE TO CELEBRATE KING GEORGE V'S SILVER JUBILEE. THEY ARE ACCOMPANIED BY THE DUKE AND DUCHESS OF KENT.

Queen Consort

'The Yorks will do it very well.'

KING GEORGE V'S DEATH was followed by a six-month official period of mourning. During this time the new King, Edward VIII, set about the task of bringing the monarchy up to date, taking a proper and serious interest in affairs of state, and gave all the appearance of settling down to the task in hand. Nevertheless, he was devastated by the death of his father and there have been suggestions that this was partly due his having already been contemplating renouncing his claim to the throne when his accession took him by surprise.

The Duchess of York too, missed her father-in-law. His sons may have found him crusty, stern, demanding and difficult to get on with, but she had established a loving and warm rapport with him. She wrote, 'I miss him dreadfully. In all the twelve years of having me as a daughter-in-law he never spoke one unkind or abrupt word to me, and was always ready to listen and give advice on one's own silly little affairs.'

The new King had been an immensely popular figure during his years as Prince of Wales. Handsome, fashionable and modern, he had been a member of the 'fast set',

HAVING GROWN UP IN THE SECURITY OF A LOVING FAMILY, QUEEN ELIZABETH VALUED THE PRECIOUS TIME THAT SHE AND THE KING COULD SPEND WITH THEIR TWO DAUGHTERS. HERE THE ENTIRE FAMILY, INCLUDING THEIR BELOVED DOGS, IS ROMPING IN THE 'LITTLE HOUSE' AT WINDSOR.

frequenting night-clubs, invariably accompanied by elegant women. People still thought indulgently of him as a 'young' man, although by this time he was over 40. His mode of life had caused his father concern and Queen Mary believed that the worry caused by his irresponsible attitude had hastened his father's death. King George himself had said, 'After I'm gone, the boy will ruin himself in twelve months.' Perhaps his undemonstrative upbringing, with its stern attention to duty, influenced the course his life would take. Whatever the reason, his fatal flaw was a weakness for married women; he had conducted a succession of affairs. In 1930 he was introduced to Wallis Simpson, an American still married to her second husband. By 1936 she was an entrenched figure, especially at Fort Belvedere, the King's Windsor residence.

It was never likely that the Duchess of York and Mrs. Simpson would have become friends, even in different circumstances. The Duchess came from a family that took its wealth for granted and that had a long-standing tradition of service and sense of duty. She was a home-loving, family-centred woman with deep religious convictions. Mrs. Simpson had the breezy sophistication typical of her own milieu and an open contempt for many of the traditions that the British establishment held dear. Although she recognized the Duchess's 'famous charm', she remained impervious to it.

It has been suggested that Mrs. Simpson met with resentment simply because she was American. This does not seem likely, for the British aristocracy had warmly embraced other transatlantic cousins: Lady Cunard, Lady Astor and the King's former mistress Lady Furness, for example. The real stumbling block was her husband – or rather both of them. She had divorced her first husband, Earl Winfield Spencer, in 1927 and at the time of the King's accession was still married to Ernest Simpson.

It is difficult nowadays to appreciate just how outrageous the idea of the King's marrying a divorcée seemed at that time – especially in the light of the widely publicized marital problems and separations that affected the younger generation of the Royal Family in the 1980s and 1990s. Queen Mary and the Duchess of York were in complete agreement that it was out of the question that a lady 'with two husbands living' could marry the King. It became increasingly apparent to the family, however, that the King was deeply in love with Mrs. Simpson. This was more than mere flirtation: marriage was on his mind. The wider public, though, knew little or nothing of the affair. Strange as it seems in these days of non-stop 'royal' stories, there was an agreement among the British press barons to keep the story out of the newspapers.

The King lost his earlier enthusiasm for hard work and became careless with state papers; they were sometimes returned from Fort Belvedere stained with wet rings from cocktail glasses. Mrs. Simpson acted as his hostess, giving orders to the domestic staff and, to the Duchess of York's stunned amazement, to the King himself. A cruise with Mrs. Simpson in the summer of 1936 was widely reported in newspapers across the world, except in Britain, causing the Royal Family and the British Government grave disquiet. The King started to include Mrs. Simpson's name in the Court Circular, and, when her divorce papers were filed at Ipswich, word began to spread.

Throughout this worrying period the Duke and Duchess continued with their public engagements, while at the same time being involved in family conferences concerning a situation that was approaching crisis point. The King certainly envied his younger brother the happiness and stability of his family life and was fond of the Duchess. For a long time she remained convinced that he would see reason. There is no record of her voicing direct, explicit criticism of Mrs. Simpson or, indeed, of the King. In fact, the records are strangely silent. Without a doubt, however, she did not believe that the King should place his personal desires above the duties of his office. Queen Mary was more outspoken and later wrote to her eldest son, 'You did not seem to take in any point of view but your own ... I do not think you have ever realised the shock which the attitude you took up caused the family.'

By mid-November, the King had informed his family that he was determined to marry Mrs. Simpson; if the only way he could achieve this was to abdicate, then he

THE DUCHESS'S SMILING SERENITY DOES NOT BETRAY
THE ALMOST INTOLERABLE STRESS AND ANXIETY WITH
WHICH SHE WAS FILLED THROUGHOUT THE DIFFICULT
YEAR OF 1936.

was prepared to do so. This provoked a flurry of Government activity. The British press could no longer remain gagged. Public debate raged – some people passionately in favour of the romance and others equally vehemently against it. On 3 December, when the Duke and Duchess of York returned from a visit to Scotland, during which she had been granted the freedom of Edinburgh, there was such uproar that they and all other members of the Royal Family had to cancel their public engagements.

The Prime Minister, Stanley Baldwin, knew by Saturday, 5 December, that the King was determined to abdicate. He asked him to delay making a public announcement. The weekend involved numerous comings and goings between the Royal Household and the ministers of the Government, during which they debated the suitability of the Duke of York to accede to the throne. Suggestions were made that his lack of self-confidence would make the undertaking too great and that his stammer might return as a major handicap. It was suggested that, with the Royal Family's agreement, the crown should pass to the Duke of Kent. This was partly because, having married Princess Marina in 1934, he had a son who could become the Prince of Wales, thus relieving little Princess Elizabeth of a 'heavy burden'.

One can only speculate on the Duchess's feelings. She undoubtedly considered the King's actions wrong and selfish, she was appalled by the prospect of her husband's accession, deeply anxious about the implications for all her family, especially for Princess Elizabeth, and angry and humiliated by suggestions that the Duke was unacceptable or unworthy. Meanwhile, she made every effort to maintain family life with the minimum of disruption and to support her husband. To make a bad situation worse, she developed influenza and was confined to bed at 145 Piccadilly.

On 10 December, the King signed the Instrument of Abdication and the next day he broadcast to the nation before leaving the country that evening. He spoke of how he felt unable to 'carry the heavy burden of responsibility' and discharge his duties as King 'without the help and support of the woman I love'. Perhaps more significantly, he also said of his brother, 'And he has one matchless blessing, enjoyed by so many of you and not bestowed on me, a happy home with his wife and children.'

In his speech at the Accession Council, the new King, George VI, began, 'With my wife and helpmeet by my side, I take up the heavy task which lies before me'. She was to remain a source of unwavering support throughout his relatively brief reign.

Queen Mary never forgave her eldest son for what she saw as his betrayal of trust and virtually refused to acknowledge the existence of Mrs. Simpson, even after she became the Duchess of Windsor. Once she had accepted the irrevocability of King Edward's decision, she said, 'The Yorks will do it very well' – tacitly expressing her appreciation and awareness of the role her daughter-in-law would be undertaking.

It was characteristic that the new Queen immediately turned her attention to the future, wasting no time on regrets. She wrote to the Archbishop of Canterbury: 'I can hardly now believe that we have been called to this tremendous task and (I am writing to you quite intimately) the curious thing is that we are not afraid. I feel that God has enabled us to face the situation calmly.' This was the first letter she signed 'Elizabeth R'. One of the King's first actions, on 14 December, his 41st birthday, was to bestow the Order of the Garter upon his wife. She wrote to her mother-in-law, 'He had discovered that Papa gave it to you on his, Papa's, birthday, 3 June, and the coincidence was so charming that he has now followed suit'.

A peaceful, traditional family Christmas at Sandringham provided a welcome respite before the demands of the New Year and the impending Coronation. The move into Buckingham Palace was a formidable enterprise and required all the Queen's energy and homemaking instincts. Her reward was the King's appreciative comment, 'Elizabeth could make a home anywhere'.

Fortunately, while still Duke of York, the King had been involved in the preparations for his brother's Coronation. The date remained unchanged – 12 May. The only alteration was that now a Queen also was to be crowned. Suggestions in the

FACING: THE DUKE AND DUCHESS OF WINDSOR WERE INVITED TO ATTEND THE CEREMONIAL UNVEILING OF A PLAQUE TO QUEEN MARY IN THE MALL IN 1967 – A SIGN THAT THE RAW WOUNDS OF THE ABDICATION HAD AT LAST HEALED.

press – some sections of which were very prejudiced against the new King – that the ceremony was to be shortened because the King would be unable to cope, must have been very hurtful. In fact, nothing was changed and the King, Queen and speech therapist Lionel Logue were hard at work behind the scenes practising and rehearsing the King's responses for this ordeal.

On the Sunday before the Coronation the Archbishop of Canterbury visited the King and Queen for private prayers. He said afterwards, 'I prayed for them and for their realm and empire and I gave them my personal blessing. I was much moved, and so were they. Indeed there were tears in their eyes when we rose from our knees.' On 11 May a state banquet was held for more than 450 guests. None of the Royal Family got very much sleep that night, as they were awoken in the early hours of the morning by the testing of the loudspeakers. The ceremony was to be broadcast, unlike the King and Queen's wedding; the idea of broadcasting that had been vetoed on the grounds that people in public houses might listen to the ceremony with their hats on!

Queen Mary broke with precedent by attending the Coronation; previously, dowager queens had always been absent. She travelled in a carriage with the Princesses Elizabeth and Margaret. The Queen was the first to enter the Abbey, moving in what was afterwards described as a 'trance of consecration'. The time-honoured ritual proceeded with few problems, none of them caused by the King's erstwhile stammer. There was some difficulty in establishing which way round the St. Edward's Crown should go and a bishop trod on the King's robes at one point, nearly causing him to take a tumble. The Queen watched her husband with loving pride and apparent serenity, taking her part in the ritual in a calm, graceful manner. She was crowned with a new crown – a tradition for a Queen Consort – made of platinum, gold and fine jewels, the most splendid of which was the Koh-i-noor diamond. Afterwards, they rode back through the cheering crowds, whose enthusiasm and excitement were unaffected by the pouring rain.

FACING: THE CORONATION CEREMONY HAD BEEN DRAINING AND TIRING. NEVERTHELESS, THE ROYAL FAMILY RESPONDED TO THE ENTHUSIASM OF THE WAITING CROWDS, DONNING THEIR HEAVY CROWNS AND APPEARING ON THE BALCONY FIVE TIMES. THEN, SO GREAT WAS THE STRESS OF THE OCCASION, THE QUEEN LOST HER VOICE AND HAD TO RETIRE TO BED.

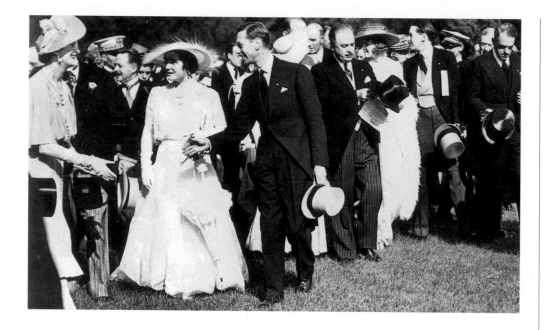

FOLLOWING LADY STRATHMORE'S DEATH A STATE VISIT TO FRANCE HAD TO BE TEMPORARILY POSTPONED. NORMAN HARTNELL HAD ALREADY DESIGNED MORE THAN 30 DRESSES FOR THE QUEEN. HIS WORKROOMS COMPLETELY REMADE THE BRILLIANTLY COLOURED FLOWING GOWNS IN WHITE, ONE OF THE THREE ACCEPTABLE ROYAL COLOURS OF MOURNING — IN JUST THREE WEEKS.

The celebrations continued throughout the week with a series of Coronation drives through London, a state banquet and a Court ball. These were followed by visits to Wales, Northern Ireland and Edinburgh, where the King invested the Queen with the Order of the Thistle.

The Queen retained all the charm and lively interest that she had shown as Duchess of York, but she acquired an additional dignity. She walked slightly more slowly, developed her famous gracious wave and, in her dress, established a personal stylishness that was beyond mere fashion.

On 22 June 1938, David Bowes Lyon telephoned the Queen to tell her that their mother had suffered a severe heart attack. The King and Queen immediately visited the Strathmores in their London home, and at 2.00 a.m. Lady Strathmore, surrounded by, her family died. A state visit to France, due to begin on 28 June, was postponed, but for only three weeks. Devastated though she was by the loss of her beloved mother, the Queen was conscientious and knew that her place must be beside the King. The spectacular four-day visit took place and the Queen captivated the French, establishing a wholly new entente cordiale.

On their return, they found London a striking contrast to the triumphant parades of Paris. Trenches were being dug in the parks, sandbags filled, gas masks issued and evacuation lists compiled; the Fleet had been mobilized. For a while, following Neville Chamberlain's notorious 'peace in our time' negotiations at Munich in September 1938, it looked as if war might be averted. It was decided, therefore, that a visit to Canada and the United States planned for May 1939 should still take place.

The Queen's part in turning the tide of American opinion about the impending war in Europe is impossible to quantify, but there is no doubt that she won enormous emotional support for her country. Passionate republicans fell under her spell. One newspaper headline said it all, 'The British re-capture Washington.' Thousands lined the streets and congregated at the stations along the railway line through the Rockies along which the King and Queen travelled. The Queen had given instructions that she was to be alerted whenever a crowd was gathering and that the train should slow down. On one occasion, late at night, she actually got out of bed, put on a dressing gown, combed her hair and put on a tiara so that she looked like the queen everyone wanted to see. She never disappointed the many people who waited for her arrival. It was on this trip that she established the informal style of chatting to the crowds, particularly the children, still followed by the Royal Family today. She also took the opportunity to set the record straight for those who felt that the abdication crisis had in any way been a slight to America because of Wallis Simpson's nationality.

The long journey home brought the King and Queen back to a Britain on the verge of war. They immediately resumed their public duties, although both must have

ABOVE: THE QUEEN ALWAYS HAD A RAPPORT WITH CHILDREN AND CLEARLY FOUND SOMETHING CHEERFUL TO SAY TO THIS GOOD-NATURED GROUP CLUSTERED ON A STACK OF OVERCROWDED BUNKS IN A DEEP SHELTER IN SOUTH LONDON.

FACING: CHARACTERISTICALLY, THE QUEEN'S FIRST COMMENT WHEN BUCKINGHAM PALACE RECEIVED A DIRECT HIT IN SEPTEMBER 1940 WAS, 'I'M ALMOST GLAD WE'VE BEEN BOMBED. I CAN NOW LOOK THE EAST END IN THE FACE.'

been tired after such an exhausting visit. In all they had travelled over 7,000 km. At 11.00 a.m. on Sunday, 3 September 1939, Britain declared war on Germany. During the next six years, the Queen would become the embodiment of British courage and endurance, as well as an inspiration to thousands in the Empire and stationed overseas. Elegantly dressed (her one venture into uniform was not, she decided, a success) and always carrying her gas mask, she visited evacuee centres, Red Cross stations, docks, ambulance trains, factories, WRENS, WAAFS and WAACS, air-raid shelters, first aid posts, fire stations. She travelled more than 8,000 km, mostly on the royal train, often sleeping in sidings overnight. Although she hated speaking on the radio, she made three moving broadcasts: to the women of the Empire on 11 November 1939, to the people of the United States on 10 August 1941 and again to the women of the Empire on 11 April 1943.

Buckingham Palace became a refugee camp for heads of state fleeing the Nazis, including King Haakon of Norway and Queen Wilhelmina of the Netherlands, who, having just been rescued from invasion, arrived in torn clothes and a tin hat. Less welcome visitors to the country – although not to the Palace except for an hour-long meeting with the King – were the Duke and Duchess of Windsor, ex-King Edward VIII and the former Mrs. Simpson. Apart from the fact that there is never an appropriate role for an ex-king, the Duke's apparent sympathies with Nazi Germany made his presence an embarrassment. He was later appointed Governor of the Bahamas where he and the Duchess spent the duration of the war.

Everyone who met the King and Queen was struck by their complete disregard of danger. It was only as a result of considerable pressure that they agreed to have a shelter installed under the Palace and the Queen simply laughed at the suggestion of a bullet-proof car. She became a frequent sight in the East End during the dark days of 1940, offering sympathy, comfort, encouragement and her own special brand of good cheer. There are dozens of stories about her actions at this time – how her eyes

glittered with tears of sympathy when told of someone's personal loss, how she knelt in the dust to persuade (successfully) a frightened dog to come out from where he was hiding in bomb debris, how she helped an injured woman dress her baby. Everywhere she went she brightened people's lives and boosted their morale. One onlooker in the East End summed up her presence: 'Oh, ain't she just bloody lovely!'

A belief in their role as the heads of the great national family was what made the King and Queen decide not to send the Princesses to safety abroad. Most other parents were unable to do so, and they believed strongly in sharing the hardships of their people. The Queen said, 'The Princesses cannot go without me. I cannot go without the King. The King will never go.' The Palace kitchens were encouraged to use powdered egg and Spam and to manage on the 'coupons'. Lights were switched off and bath water was strictly rationed.

When V.E. Day came in May 1945, the crowds surged around Buckingham Palace and called again and again for the Royal Family to come out on the balcony. Forty years later Queen Elizabeth II recalled the occasion. 'My mother had put her tiara on for the occasion, so we asked my parents if we could go out and see for ourselves. Down in the crowds we cheered the King and Queen and then walked miles through the streets. Coming back, we stood outside the Palace and shouted "We want the King!" and were successful in seeing my parents on the balcony yet again at midnight. I think it was one of the most memorable moments of my life.'

The war had taken its toll on the entire nation, including the King and Queen. His brother the Duke of Kent had been killed in a flying boat accident on a secret mission to Iceland in 1942. The Queen's nephew Captain John Patrick Bowes-Lyon had been killed in action in 1941; in addition, her elderly father had died in 1944. Many of the places that the King and Queen both loved had been destroyed in the bombing. This was, however, a time for looking forward and building a new future, in spite of the strict austerity still in force throughout the country.

ABOVE: THROUGHOUT THE WEEK-LONG CELEBRATIONS OF VE DAY, CROWDS BESIEGED BUCKINGHAM PALACE, CALLING REPEATEDLY FOR THE KING AND QUEEN.

FACING: THE ROYAL FAMILY EPITOMIZED THE BRITISH WARTIME SLOGAN 'BUSINESS AS USUAL'.

THE KING AND QUEEN WERE BOTH ANXIOUS TO
SPEND TIME WITH THEIR DAUGHTERS FOLLOWING THE
HECTIC EARLY DAYS OF THEIR REIGN AND THE EVEN
MORE CHAOTIC DAYS OF THE WAR.

During the war years the two princesses had grown up, and their parents were fully aware that they had both missed many of the normal pleasures that they could otherwise have expected. In September 1945 the family took a well-deserved holiday in Balmoral and returned to London refreshed. Nevertheless, people began to note how strained and tired the King appeared.

In 1947 the entire family made a tour of southern Africa. It was enormously enjoyable but also very gruelling. Princess Elizabeth celebrated her 21st birthday in South Africa, giving a broadcast in which she dedicated herself to the peoples of the Commonwealth, little realizing how soon she would be called upon to fulfil her promise. Also on this tour, Princess Margaret formed a close friendship with Peter Townsend, one of the King's aides. On their return to London in May, the King joked that they had all lost weight because the visit had been so strenuous. To the Queen's increasing anxiety, it became apparent that he, at least, had grown noticeably thinner. He was also suffering from a persistent cough and attacks of cramp.

However, two months later, much happier royal concerns occupied everyone's attention. On 10 July, Buckingham Palace announced the engagement of Princess Elizabeth to Prince Philip, now simply known as plain Lieutenant Philip Mountbatten. Rapturous crowds gathered at Buckingham Palace to cheer the young couple and the King and Queen.

Even more gathered on the day of the wedding, 20 November 1947. The Royal Family felt that an ostentatious wedding would be inappropriate while the nation was still struggling to recover from the war, so the occasion was, by royal standards, somewhat muted. It was, nevertheless, a cause for great rejoicing and celebration for ordinary people as well as for the King and Queen. The King wrote to his daughter, while she was at Broadlands (the Mountbatten estate) on her honeymoon, 'I have watched you grow up all these years with pride under the skilful direction of Mummy who, as you know, is the most marvellous person in the world in my eyes...'.

'IT IS WITH THE GREATEST PLEASURE THAT THE KING AND QUEEN ANNOUNCE THE BETROTHAL OF THEIR DEARLY BELOVED DAUGHTER THE PRINCESS ELIZABETH TO LIEUTENANT PHILIP MOUNTBATTEN, R.N., SON OF THE LATE PRINCE ANDREW OF GREECE AND PRINCESS ANDREW (PRINCESS ALICE OF BATTENBERG), TO WHICH UNION THE KING HAS GLADLY GIVEN HIS CONSENT.'

FACING: THE QUEEN TOOK A HAND IN SUPERVISING MANY OF THE DETAILS OF HER ELDER DAUGHTER'S WEDDING. HER EXPRESSION OF HAPPINESS AND PRIDE REVEALED IN THIS FAMILY PHOTOGRAPH AT BUCKINGHAM PALACE IS LIKE THAT OF ANY BRIDE'S MOTHER ON SUCH A SPECIAL OCCASION.

The following year marked the King and Queen's Silver Wedding, which he decided to mark with a day of thanksgiving and rededication. Once again, this became an opportunity for thousands of ordinary people to express their loyalty and affection for the King and Queen. They were cheered throughout the drive to St. Paul's Cathedral and, on their return, called out on to the balcony again and again. Both King and Queen broadcast to the nation, speaking almost as one voice. Both expressed their dedication to continuing service to the country in the future.

The future, however, is something that even kings cannot control. The year 1948 brought an equal mixture of pain and pleasure. Princess Elizabeth gave birth to her first child, Prince Charles, on 14 November. At the same time, however, the King was seriously ill. Earlier in the year his doctors has diagnosed arteriosclerosis, and there was a risk that they might have to amputate his right foot or even his leg. The Queen moved, apparently serenely and untroubled, from one wing of the Palace to the other, from her husband to her daughter, concerned not to worry the latter. We can only guess at her inner turmoil. She also took the King's place on a number of official occasions that he was too ill to attend. He recovered sufficiently to allay the family's worst fears. In June 1949 Princess Elizabeth rode at the head of the parade for the Trooping the Colour ceremony, while the King rode in an open carriage to watch.

The King's health seemed to improve and he continued to attend assiduously to state papers and other royal 'business'. A second grandchild, Princess Anne, was born on 15 August 1950. Later in the month, the family celebrated Princess Margaret's 21st birthday at Balmoral, but only a short time afterwards the King fell seriously ill again. The doctors diagnosed cancer, and, although the Queen insisted on knowing the truth, the King was not told. On 23 September, surgeons removed his left lung. Prayers for his recovery were said throughout the Empire. The most fervent of these were the Queen's, her sustaining faith allowing her to place her trust in God. Three months later, prayers were said in thanksgiving for the King's apparent recovery.

However, the Queen knew that his recovery could be only temporary. Few outward signs of her concern and grief showed. She continued to undertake numerous official duties, reassuring people of the King's health. She also redoubled her support of her husband, keeping his morale as high as possible. Only the small inner circle of those intimately involved with Royal Family had any inkling of the extraordinary courage she showed at this time.

Christmas 1951 was spent, as always, at Sandringham. The King and Queen returned briefly to London to say good-bye to Princess Elizabeth and the Duke of Edinburgh, who were embarking on a major foreign tour. The Princess and her husband left for East Africa on 31 January. The King and Queen returned to Sandringham to rejoin Princess Margaret and their two grandchildren.

The King, with a special electrically heated waistcoat and a light gun, managed to enjoy some shooting, and spent Tuesday, 5 February engaged in this, his favourite sport. In the evening, Princess Margaret played the piano and the family listened to the radio news to hear of Princess Elizabeth's progress in Africa. The King went to bed and a drink of hot cocoa was brought to him at 11.00 p.m. One of the watchmen heard him close his bedroom window at midnight. When his valet came to call him at 7.30 a.m. on 6 February, the King was dead.

The new Queen returned at once to London and then joined her family at Sandringham. The King's body was taken on 11 February to London, where it lay in state for four days before he was buried at Windsor. Among the mourners was the Duke of Windsor, who had found the burden of kingship 'intolerable'. It is hard to imagine his sister-in-law's feelings as she bade farewell to her beloved Bertie.

ABOVE: THREE QUEENS MOURN THE DEATH OF A KING. THEIR MAJESTIES QUEEN ELIZABETH II, QUEEN MARY AND QUEEN ELIZABETH THE QUEEN MOTHER ATTEND THE FUNERAL OF KING GEORGE VI IN FEBRUARY 1952.

FACING: TWO DEVOTED GRANDPARENTS CELEBRATE PRINCE CHARLES'S THIRD BIRTHDAY. THE QUEEN'S WISDOM AND GUIDANCE WERE OF LONG-LASTING IMPORTANCE FOR THE NEXT GENERATION OF THE ROYAL FAMILY.

Queen Mother

'My only wish now is that I may be allowed to continue to do the work that we sought to do together.'

SOON AFTER THE KING'S DEATH, his widow let it be known that she wished to be styled Queen Elizabeth the Queen Mother. This was in part a practical decision to avoid any confusion between two Queen Elizabeths, but it also stemmed from her readiness to undertake yet another new role of service to the nation and to royal duty. She made her intentions clear: 'My only wish is that I may be allowed to continue to do the work that we sought to do together.' She could have had no idea that in the course of the next five decades, she would become affectionately known as the 'Queen Mum' and that she would create for herself a unique position in the life of the nation and occupy a very special place in its heart.

To begin with, the Queen Mother remained in the apartments that she and the King had occupied at Buckingham Palace, while the Queen, the Duke of Edinburgh and their family lived in the Belgian Suite on another floor. In the month before the Coronation in 1953, the Queen Mother and Princess Margaret moved to Clarence House, which remained her official London residence for the rest of her life.

FACING: NO OTHER MEMBER OF THE ROYAL FAMILY INSPIRED SUCH LASTING AFFECTION. ON HER 85TH BIRTHDAY, THE PETITE FIGURE OF THE QUEEN MOTHER IS ALMOST COMPLETELY CONCEALED BY CROWDS OF WELL-WISHERS OF ALL AGES.

There was some speculation that the Queen Mother would withdraw from public life. Many earlier dowager queens had done so, and it must have been a difficult period of adjustment from Queen Consort to Queen Mother, especially while she was still coming to terms with her private loss. Those who thought that this would be her course of her action, however, did not know her very well. Public calls on her time continued; she made her first official appearance after the King's death as early as May 1952, when she travelled to Fife to inspect the 1st Battalion of the Black Watch, of which she was Colonel-in-Chief, on the eve of their departure for Korea.

Not long afterwards, while visiting some friends in Scotland, she learned of the sale of Barrowgill Castle in Caithness. Feeling the need for privacy – and, indeed, a proper home of her own – the Queen Mother bought the weather-beaten near-ruin. She explained, 'It was a lovely little castle which was in danger of becoming derelict.' With loving care, she restored it – and its ancient name, the Castle of Mey. The planning and work on the castle also served as a restorative for her spirits. It became a refuge when she required solitude and, far more often, a place where she could offer hospitality to family and friends. The latter included many of the local people, not just dignitaries, who enjoyed the easy, friendly informality of dinner with her.

Her role as Queen Mother was her longest and final public role and the one for which she is best remembered. It would take a large volume, rather than a single chapter, even to outline the many events – public and private, official and personal, happy and sad – that filled those last bustling and ever-changing decades.

The first important event – a sad one – was the death of Queen Mary at the age of 86, on 24 March 1953. A stern and unyielding figure, she had inspired respect and admiration more than love, but the Queen Mother had grown very close to her. The two people whose guidance she had relied upon throughout her royal life had died within a little over a year of each other. This now placed the Queen Mother in the role of senior adviser to the Queen and other members of the Royal Family.

ABOVE: FROM 1957, THE QUEEN MOTHER TRAVELLED TIRELESSLY. IT IS DIFFICULT TO BELIEVE THAT THIS SPARKLING FIGURE WAS NEARLY 58 AND HAD ALREADY SPENT A GRUELLING DAY IN SYDNEY, AUSTRALIA IN A TEMPERATURE OF 30°C.

FACING: THE ROYAL FAMILY ON THE PALACE BALCONY ON CORONATION DAY, 2 JUNE 1953.

FACING TOP: ROYAL LODGE WAS ALWAYS A PLACE WHERE THE FAMILY COULD ESCAPE SOME OF THE FORMALITIES OF ROYAL LIFE, AND THE 'LITTLE HOUSE' WAS A FAVOURITE PLACE TO PLAY. HERE THE QUEEN MOTHER AND FOUR-YEAR-OLD PRINCE CHARLES PEEP THROUGH THE WINDOWS.

FACING CENTRE: A DELIGHTED GRANDMOTHER CUDDLES THE NEW BABY – PRINCE ANDREW – WHILE PRINCE CHARLES AND PRINCESS ANNE LOOK ON.

FACING BOTTOM: THE QUEEN MOTHER ALWAYS SEEMED TO ENJOY, HERSELF WHATEVER SHE WAS DOING, BUT THERE IS NO DOUBT THAT A TRIP TO THE RACES SCORED HIGHLY AMONG HER PLEASURES.

A little over two months later, following the precedent set by Queen Mary, she attended her daughter's Coronation. The occasion must have been tinged with poignancy as she remembered her own and the King's Coronation. Resplendently dressed and bejewelled, she was still indisputably a Queen as she took her place in the front row of the Royal Gallery at Westminster Abbey. Afterwards the Royal Family appeared on the balcony of Buckingham Palace, and it was a very special moment when the Duke of Edinburgh turned and led out the Queen Mother. The cheering redoubled and the applause even drowned the sound of the flypast overhead.

That sound of pure delight reverberated down the succeeding years everywhere she went. When she was asked to visit the United States in 1954, her modest response was, 'Who is going to be interested in the middle-aged widow of a King?' Nevertheless, she agreed to go and, needless to say, the visit was a tremendous success. The presentation was televised and watched by millions of Americans. One newspaper described the occasion in these words: 'The royal lady with the peaches-and-cream complexion and twinkling eyes not only drew a record crowd of 2,800 smart-setters to the Waldorf-Astoria ballroom; she sent them away humming "God Save the Queen" like a first-night audience whistling the top tunes of the hit show.'

One of the more worrying concerns of the 1950s was what became known as the 'Townsend Affair'. It is difficult now to understand what all the fuss was about; even at the time, many people's sympathies lay with the Princess. She had formed a close association with Group Captain Peter Townsend while he was member of the King's Household. The relationship deepened, and shortly after the Coronation the couple informed the Queen Mother that they wished to marry. He had previously divorced his wife, and, although he was the 'innocent party', it was unthinkable that the Queen's sister should marry a man who had been through the divorce courts.

Peter Townsend was then a member of the Queen Mother's personal staff at Clarence House. Princess Margaret required the monarch's consent to marry and the

Queen was in something of a dilemma. Head of the Church of England and with strong personal religious convictions, she also deeply sympathized with her sister. Similarly the Queen Mother appreciated her daughter's feelings, although for her the moral choice was much clearer. In any case, the Prime Minister believed that the country would not accept the marriage and the Queen was constitutionally bound to accept his advice. However, he did suggest that the couple should wait two years until the Princess was 25, when she would be able to marry without the Queen's consent.

Peter Townsend was immediately sent to Brussels, where he took up the position of air attaché to the British Embassy. The Queen Mother and the Princess embarked on a planned tour of Southern Rhodesia (now Zimbabwe), which, ironically, would originally have included the Group Captain. The couple continued to write to each other regularly and frequently with the Queen Mother's full knowledge.

Unlike the situation in 1936, the press ran stories, jokes and cartoons about the affair. Speculation reached fever pitch as 21 August 1955, Princess Margaret's 25th birthday, approached. This was extremely painful for all the family. Such was public interest that people even went on day trips in coach parties to watch the Princess going to church on Sunday morning. The press began to take a very pompous stand over the matter, The Times even going so far as to state, 'The Princess will be entering into a union which vast numbers of her sister's people ... cannot in all conscience regard as a marriage...'. Some of the tabloids were simultaneously nauseatingly salacious and sanctimonious. The Queen Mother, however, while firm in her own moral standpoint concerning both royal responsibility and the sanctity of marriage and the family, wisely left her daughter to make up her own mind. Peter Townsend later wrote, 'The Queen Mother was never anything but considerate in her attitude to me, to us both, throughout the whole difficult affair'.

On 31 October Princess Margaret issued a statement in which she explained her decision not to marry Group Captain Townsend. The couple did meet again in 1958,

when Peter Townsend was hospitably welcomed by the Queen Mother at Clarence House. Princess Margaret married Antony Armstrong-Jones in 1960. Some 23 years after issuing her statement about the 'Townsend Affair' Princess Margaret divorced Lord Snowdon. There was little, if any, public disapproval. Far from showing disapprobation, the Queen Mother remained lovingly close to her younger daughter. No doubt she was saddened; any mother would be. Not only was she always the soul of discretion, but she had a realistic attitude, wasting no time with regrets over the past but facing up to the present and looking forward to the future.

Family traumas notwithstanding, the royal round continued. Even in her seventies and eighties, the Queen Mother continued to carry out a formidable number of public engagements and, until the mid-1970s, to travel virtually around the world. Among her favourite duties was her role as Chancellor of London University, a responsibility she did not relinquish until 1980. Tirelessly, she visited colleges, halls of residence, boat houses, formal ceremonies at the Senate House headquarters, charity balls and, of course, the long degree awards ceremony held each year at the Royal Albert Hall.

Another much-treasured office was Warden of the Cinque Ports – she was officially installed as Lord Warden on 1 August 1979. This is a historic office, which in the past was of vital military concern to the nation. Nowadays, purely honorary, it has been held in modern times by various eminent figures, including Sir Winston Churchill. The Queen Mother was not only the first royal Warden, but the first woman.

Gradually, over the years, the Queen Mother's official responsibilities were lessened. As a younger generation of the Royal Family grew up and married, the burden of public and official duties could be passed on to stronger shoulders. She had set them a standard of assiduous attention, dynamic energy and exceptional selflessness. Few have matched it.

However, if she undertook fewer official duties, she never ceased to be a focus of affection – everybody's favourite granny. For example, the spontaneous arrival of

A FAMOUS DANCER IN HER YOUTH, THE QUEEN
MOTHER STILL CUT AN ELEGANT FIGURE AT THE
UNIVERSITY OF LONDON BALL IN 1958.

children carrying bunches of garden flowers to Clarence House on her birthday quickly became a tradition. The Queen Mother warmly welcomed them, mingling informally and chatting to sometimes quite overawed small citizens. In later years, younger members of the Royal Family also attended to help gather up the huge numbers of bouquets which one elderly lady could not possibly hold.

If there is one interest or hobby that was pre-eminently associated with the Queen Mother, it must be steeplechasing. Her love of horses dated back to her country upbringing and the beloved Bobs of her early childhood. Although flat racing has always been regarded as the 'sport of kings' and was enjoyed by the Queen Mother, she was persuaded by Lord Mildmay to take an interest in 'chasers'. In 1949, together with Princess Elizabeth, she bought her first steeplechaser. She developed an interest in and knowledge of the sport that became the envy of many acknowledged experts. She became, in her own word, 'hooked' on steeplechasing. She was never happier than the times spent on the race course, particularly in the paddock, chatting to trainer and jockey. She formed a close friendship with Major Peter Cazalet who trained many of her finest horses and was deeply saddened by his death in 1973. The entire racing fraternity acknowledged her understanding and extensive knowledge of the sport and of horses and her 'sporting' attitude was legendary.

One of the Queen Mother's most important roles was as adviser and guide to the younger generation of the Royal Family throughout difficult and rapidly changing times. She was especially close to Prince Charles, whose romance with Lady Diana Spencer was a special joy to her, partly because of her warm and long-standing friendship with the Spencer family. Even more importantly, she knew, if anyone did, the value of a loving and supportive marriage, particularly in the stressful public world of the British monarchy. Indeed, before her wedding, Lady Diana Spencer stayed with the Queen Mother to 'learn the ropes'. It must have been a great grief to the Queen Mother when the Prince and Princess of Wales acknowledged, some 12

years after their fairy-tale wedding, their marriage had failed. At the time, though, the Queen Mother announced that Diana was 'perfect for him,' and was overjoyed to see the couple so happy in their early days. She felt confident that the future of the monarchy was intact, taking Diana under her wing and providing the young princess with advice that would help her through the minefields of protocol.

Soon afterwards, Andrew, Charles's younger brother, married the lively Sarah Ferguson, quickly dubbed 'Fergie'. The Queen Mother had always had a soft spot for Prince Andrew because of his high spirits and 'get-up-and-go' style. He reminded her very much of herself as a child. And, despite her antics, which occasionally provoked reproof, Fergie also became a favourite with the Queen Mother. However, as much as she enjoyed the energy and enthusiasm of the 'new royals', the Queen Mother was, above all, concerned about the dignity of the Royal Family, and she cautioned its younger members when she felt they had gone too far. The lavish holidays of the Yorks, and their £3.5 million new home, for example, caused her concern in a time when the nation was deep in recession. As always, she felt the actions of Royal Family should reflect the mood of the people, and provide them with a noble and trustworthy role model.

The Queen Mother had always been perceptive and it was not long before she became aware of the frayed relationship between Charles and Diana. She was so concerned that she confided her worries to her daughter, the Queen, who decided against interfering in what she considered to be a personal affair. It must have caused the Queen Mother immense sorrow when the Prince and Princess of Wales publicly acknowledged their marital difficulties. She must, too, have been saddened by other marital problems among her grandchildren and other members of the Royal Family. Although her own life was untouched by scandal, she never voiced public criticism of any of the young royals. Her own standards were impeccable, but she was remarkable for her tolerance of other people's failings.

The Princess Royal was also divorced in the same year that the Yorks separated and the Prince and Princess of Wales went their separate ways. The Queen Mother steeled herself to

With undiminished zest and vitality, the Queen Mother smiles serenely as crowds gather to celebrate her 94th birthday. Family members sharing this special occasion span four generations and include the Queen, a surprisingly adult Prince William, the Princess Royal and her second husband, Tim Lawrence.

attend the Princess's second marriage eight months later (neither the Princess of Wales nor the Duchess of York attended), but it required a good deal of courage. One of her ladies-in-waiting noted, 'She's very upset about the divorces and separations. She's very upset but she definitely thinks the monarchy under Charles will continue. I don't think she would ever contemplate it not. She's a great royalist'.

The Queen announced publicly that 1992 had been an *annus horribilis*, and indeed the problems of the younger royals had thrown the first shadow of the guillotine over the House of Windsor. The Prince and Princess of Wales had been icons, and many believed that they would guarantee the monarchy's survival. The Queen Mother made no public comment about the family dramas. Two of the three great crises in her life had involved marriage and divorce; the third not only involved her favourite grandson, but threatened her whole way of life.

The Queen Mother continued to set an example to the younger royals, each of whom benefited from her sense of duty and her capacity for hard work. She remained a figure of unerring honour and integrity, and when the monarchy struggled through its most difficult years of crisis in the years leading up to and after Princess Diana's death, the Queen Mother reserved judgement and continued to represent her family and everything for which it stood as she had always done.

The Queen herself remains unflinching in her devotion to her country, and although more reserved than her mother, has proved throughout the last decade that the Royal Family can still unite the nation. She has held together the strings of what often appeared to be a disintegrating institution, and with ingenuity, determination and a real sense of pride in her country and its people, has shown that she can take the monarchy into the twenty-first century, and give it new meaning in the lives of coming generations. If her Court has failed to follow through the vision and initiatives of her mother – the first successful 'outsider' ever to penetrate royal circles – it has weathered storms that would have been unimaginable only a decade ago.

PRINCE CHARLES AND PRINCESS DIANA, SHORTLY BEFORE THEIR SEPARATION WAS ANNOUNCED; DESPITE THE GRIEF SHE FELT FOR THE BREAKUP OF THEIR MARRIAGE, THE QUEEN MOTHER CONTINUED TO SUPPORT HER GRANDSON THROUGH THE DIFFICULT TIMES.

Her battle has undoubtedly been aided by the presence and continued support of her mother. No member of the Royal Family has ever given so much innocent and charming pleasure to so many people over such an unbelievable length of time. At the Service of Thanksgiving for her 80th birthday, the Archbishop of Canterbury could not have recalled a more appropriate remark than the one made by the first Queen Elizabeth: 'Though God hath raised me high, yet this I count the glory of my crown; that I have reigned with your loves.'

The Queen Mother carved a unique and special niche in the hearts of the people the world over – in particular those who witnessed her devoted work throughout the Second World War. The VE Celebrations of 1995 erupted into rapturous applause when the Queen Mother appeared on the balcony of Buckingham Palace with her daughters. As she wiped away a tear, the country was reminded of that day, fifty years earlier, when she stood beside her husband, King George VI, with the crowd chanting, 'We want the King!'.

Indeed, *The Times* wrote: 'Yesterday, on the anniversary of VE-Day, it was for the Queen Mother that the vast crowds gathered outside Buckingham Palace. With the passing of a generation of wartime leaders, she remains a living link to those terrible times. Her courage and serenity then inspired the nation; her steadfast endurance now commands the love and respect of a generation not yet born when she came out on the balcony of Buckingham Palace in 1945. Churchill told the crowds then: "This is your victory." Yesterday, it was hers.'

Later in the celebrations, the Queen Mother broke a long silence to address the people. With confidence and quiet dignity she said: 'This day will bring back many memories to many people. I do hope that all those who go to the many ceremonies will remember with pride and gratitude the men and women, armed and unarmed, whose courage really helped to bring us victory. God bless them all.' Thunderous cheers greeted her words, paying tribute to her remarkable courage and dedication to duty – and to her own great losses and staunch determination to carry through 'with the people'. She modestly waved her acknowledgement, perhaps unaware of the fact that she may have saved the monarchy for a second time.

ABOVE: THE EMOTION OF THE VE DAY ANNIVERSARY CELEBRATIONS IN 1995 CAUGHT UP WITH THE QUEEN MOTHER AS SHE CAME ON TO THE BALCONY AT BUCKINGHAM PALACE TO GREET THE CROWDS.

FACING: THE QUEEN MOTHER AND HER FAVOURITE GRANDSON, PRINCE CHARLES, WAVE CHEERFULLY TO THE CROWDS GATHERED OUTSIDE THE ESTATE AT SANDRINGHAM.

THE PRINCE OF WALES HAS ALWAYS BEEN
PARTICULARLY CLOSE TO HIS GRANDMOTHER,
WHO, WITH LOVE AND COMPASSION, INSTILLED IN
HIM THE SENSE OF DUTY SHE BELIEVED TO BE
THE GREAT STRENGTH OF THE MONARCHY.

Prince Charles, too, has followed his grandmother's example by trying to put aside personal problems to take an interest in the lives of the ordinary people. Closer to his grandmother than his mother, he has inherited many of her traits, including a natural geniality and a talent for making people laugh. The Queen Mother was constantly aware that one day Prince Charles would be King, and she helped instill in him, as gently but firmly as possible, that he must face his duties. Years later, Prince Charles wrote: 'Ever since I can remember, my grandmother has been the most wonderful example of fun, laughter, warmth, infinite security and, above all else, exquisite taste. For me she has always been one of those extraordinarily rare people whose touch can turn everything into gold.' The Queen Mother later came to accept that Prince Charles's marriage was injured beyond repair, and although she felt sympathy for Diana, she made it clear where her loyalties lay. She had no choice but to side with Charles.

Although the Princess and the Queen Mother had grown apart in the years following the divorce, she never ceased to feel for the troubled young woman and she had formed a strong and lasting relationship with her grandsons, Princes William and Harry. Princess Diana was in many ways a modern incarnation of the Queen Mother, and it is no coincidence that the press christened them both the 'Queen of Hearts'. They shared the same natural flair for royal work, with a dedication to the causes of the people and a warmth of spirit that touched the hearts of many.

When the death of Princess Diana was announced at the first light of dawn on 31 August 1997, a shock wave of grief stretched around the globe. Thousands of messages and tributes were lovingly placed at the gates of Buckingham Palace and Diana's home in Kensington Palace, and the Royal Family undoubtedly drew great comfort from the unimaginable public support and love for the beautiful young Princess. There had been much public criticism of the Royal Family for remaining in Balmoral and not returning to London immediately after the Princess's death. In a dramatic move, the Queen bowed to public pressure and returned to London a day earlier than planned. Her presence in the capital, and

ABOVE: THE QUEEN MOTHER WITH PRINCE ANDREW AND THE DUCHESS OF YORK AT THE CHRISTMAS DAY SERVICE IN NORFOLK IN 1988, IN THE HAPPY DAYS BEFORE THE MARITAL DIFFICULTIES OF THE YOUNGER ROYALS CAME TO LIGHT.

LEFT: THE MARRIAGE OF PRINCE EDWARD TO SOPHIE RHYS-JONES IN JUNE 1999 BROUGHT MUCH HAPPINESS TO THE QUEEN MOTHER, WHO APPROVED OF THE FAMILY SPIRIT OF THE OCCASION.

PRINCE ANDREW PRESENTS HIS GRANDMOTHER
WITH A BOUQUET OF FLOWERS AS SHE WAITS TO
GREET WELL-WISHERS ON HER 97TH BIRTHDAY.

her televised speech, in which she described Diana as an 'exceptional and gifted human being' helped to unite the grief-stricken nation.

On the day of the funeral, the crowds watched in silence as the Queen and the Queen Mother joined the millions of mourners on the streets in front of Buckingham Palace – an unprecedented tribute to the 'people's princess'. More telling, perhaps, they dispensed with royal protocol, after a period of somewhat bitter debate, and flew the flag on Buckingham Palace at half-mast. Even in her 97th year, the Queen Mother showed strength, compassion and dignity, hiding her heartbreak behind a weak smile as she made her way up the steps of Westminster Abbey, and leaning heavily on her stick. She was no stranger to sorrow, having lost a brother and a beloved husband, but the tragedy of the young Princess made this one of the saddest days of her life.

The marriage of her youngest grandchild, Prince Edward, to Sophie Rhys-Jones in June 1999 brought a new and particular joy to the Queen Mother, after the marital crises of the young royals in the early years of the 1990s and the death of Diana, Princess of Wales. Although the service, held at Windsor Castle, lacked the pomp and circumstance of previous royal weddings, the Queen Mother's happiness was evident as she smiled and waved at the crowds before she entered the chapel. It was very much a family occasion, with most close members of the Royal Family attending. The spirit of the occasion was one with which the Queen Mother wholeheartedly agreed. The events of the past decade had proved that a lavish public wedding did not necessarily make for a happy and lasting marriage.

It seemed to many that the Queen Mother would go on for ever. She had such extraordinary resilience, it was difficult to believe that she could be older than the century – even if only by five months. Until the 1990s her itinerary gave the impression of a hectic succession of commitments not possible to fulfil by other women of her age. And even after the regular appearances began to wind down, she continued to appear in support of her family, the causes she held dear to her heart, and the nation to which she had devoted the better part of her life.

EVEN IN HER NINETIES, THE QUEEN MOTHER CONTINUED HER PUBLIC APPEARANCES, ALWAYS ENJOYING THE OPPORTUNITY TO MEET HER YOUNG FANS.

She was blessed with generally good health, although throughout her life she was prone to throat and lung infections. On the rare occasions that she was ill, she made little fuss and tried to avoid disappointing people who were looking forward to seeing her. She had an instinctive distaste for disease, and fortunately experienced less physical unpleasantness than many women of her age. Her appendix was removed in 1964 and she made an almost immediate recovery. She then spent three weeks in the Caribbean, supposedly convalescing; in fact, she visited 12 different islands – virtually a small Royal Tour. In 1966 she had a colostomy, a painful operation, and for the next 13 years this was euphemistically referred to as the Queen Mother's 'major abdominal surgery'. It was later admitted that she had undergone a colostomy, and many men and women have been encouraged to have the operation on the basis that the Queen Mother herself had done so and gone on to have a healthy and fulfilling life.

Anyone visiting her as she recuperated in hospital would have found it difficult to believe that she had undergone such a serious operation. She remained in exceptionally good spirits, did not complain, and welcomed all the thousands of good wishes with her usual charm.

In the first decade of her widowhood, the Queen Mother was prone to stumbling, and suffered a series of accidents that threatened her normal good health, and her indomitable spirit. In 1956 she fell at Clarence House and twisted her ankle. In 1960 she knocked her leg at the Royal Lodge. In 1961 she fell during an Ascot house party at Windsor and broke a bone in her foot, and in 1962 she stumbled at Birkhall and broke it again. She seemed to have recovered her footing until just before her grandson's wedding in 1981, when she ran a high temperature. After similar mishaps in her nineties she walked with a stick, and her right leg was almost permanently bandaged.

Not surprisingly, some of her falls were more serious, and she underwent surgery for a hip replacement in her mid-nineties. Her recovery was, as usual, remarkable, and after several weeks of visits from her family, she began to make regular appearances once again. In January 1998, the Queen Mother fell once again at Sandringham, and underwent emergency

LEFT: THE QUEEN MOTHER RECEIVES A BRITISH FLAG FROM ONE OF HER MANY THOUSANDS OF ADMIRERS AS SHE CELEBRATES HER 95TH BIRTHDAY.

OVERLEAF: THE EPITOME OF CHARM, SOPHISTICATION, COMPASSION AND DEVOTION, THE QUEEN MOTHER WAS THE SYMBOL OF WHAT THE ROYAL FAMILY SHOULD REPRESENT FOR MORE THAN 70 YEARS.

OVERLEAF: THE QUEEN MOTHER,
ACCOMPANIED BY PRINCE CHARLES, VISITS THE
SANDRIMGHAM FLOWER SHOW IN 1997.

RIGHT: THE QUEEN MOTHER ALWAYS TOOK A
PERSONAL AND GENUINE INTEREST IN THE
CAUSES SHE SUPPORTED; HERE AT THE
TWENTIETH ANNIVERSARY OF THE OPENING OF
CYNTHIA SPENCER HOUSE.

surgery to replace her second hip. Her 23-day stay in hospital was longer than predicted, and there was great public concern about her condition. Prince Andrew and Prince Charles visited their grandmother at the King Edward VII Hospital for Officers in London, and the Queen, too, made a series of visits, kept to a minimum, however, by her mother's distaste for fuss. One royal source explained that the Queen Mother had been adamant that she would not leave the hospital until she could do so confidently – and unaided – on her own two feet. She did just that. The sudden appearance of a wheelchair ramp at the main entrance to the hospital suggested that the royal recovery might yet be some way off. But this was for another homebound patient. Shortly after eleven in the morning, the doors opened and into the bright sunlight came King Edward VII's determined granddaughter-in-law. With two sticks clutched in one hand, she used the other to wave to the cameras. The hospital matron hovered close for the short descent to the royal Daimler, but the Queen Mother used only the banister for support, and graciously accepted a bouquet as she reached her car.

Flowers in one hand, sticks in the other, the solo routine continued. As the car sped off, she remained upright on the edge of her seat to wave to well-wishers. Her discharge came as a surprise to the Prince of Wales as he toured Bristol. 'She is amazing,' he said. 'She is doing wonderfully.'

For many thousands of people, the Queen Mother's death was a personal loss and, because of her remarkable courage and enduring will to live, a shock. A matriarch of compassion, she had shared the nation's triumphs and sorrows, both in wartime and in peace – often providing the leadership and example for those around her to follow. Men and women from all walks of life have been inspired and encouraged by her strength of character and her unerring warmth. She was the first royal to display the 'common touch', becoming its favourite member and undoubtedly its linchpin. While the Royal Family has come under increasing attack, the Queen Mother herself has remained the symbol of what the monarchy should represent. After more than 70 years of devoted service to her country, it is arguable that this invincible woman may have been the most loved person in the Western World. From

EVEN IN HER FINAL YEARS, THE QUEEN MOTHER REGULARLY ATTENDED TRADITIONAL ROYAL EVENTS; HERE SHE LEAVES THE CHAPEL AT WINDSOR CASTLE AFTER THE EASTER SERVICE IN 1998, ACCOMPANIED BY THE DUKE OF EDINBURGH AND PRINCE ANDREW.

the carefree days of her Scottish aristocratic birth and young girlhood, to the dazzle of entering the Royal Family – to the huge public role she occupied until her death, the Queen Mother emerged as an entrancing, enchanting and wildly popular figure. It is impossible to overestimate the true admiration and respect felt for the Queen Mother by the nation. She lived through one of the most turbulent centuries in history; she lived through war and peace, times of great joy and disaster. She faced every difficult situation – personal or national – with a courage and fortitude that could not help but inspire others. She shared in every moment of national pride and success with genuine happiness. Despite a long life spent in the public eye, she never failed to express her pleasure at the appreciation of her fans and well-wishers, and she never disappointed them. She was without question a woman of considerable sophistication and spirit, whom all the royal scandals, from the Abdication to the divorce of the Prince and Princess of Wales, left unscathed.

Everyone who met her – and even people who were simply part of a crowd gathered to see her – has a story about her charm, her kindness and her vitality. She gave people a sense of continuity and principle in a shifting moral world. Most of all, she sparkled as brightly as the diamonds in her tiara, and brought the true magic of royalty into everyday lives.

THE TRAGIC DEATH ON 9 FEBRUARY 2002,
OF HER YOUNGEST DAUGHTER, PRINCESS
MARGARET, WAS A TERRIBLE BLOW FOR THE
QUEEN MOTHER. PAINFULLY, THE DAY OF THE
FUNERAL COINCIDED WITH THE 50TH ANNIVERSARY
OF THE FUNERAL OF HER LATE HUSBAND. WITH
GREAT COURAGE, THE QUEEN MOTHER ATTENDED
THE PRIVATE CEREMONY AT ST GEORGE'S CHAPEL
WITH THE ROYAL FAMILY AND 400 OTHER
MOURNERS. WHEN THE QUEEN MOTHER WAS
DRIVEN AWAY IT WAS THE LAST TIME
THE PUBLIC SAW HER.

After her death, The Queen Mother's devoted grandson, The Prince of Wales, paid a special tribute to her which touched the nation:

'I know what my darling grandmother meant to so many other people. She literally enriched their lives, and she was the original life enhancer, whether publicly or privately, whoever she was with. And in many ways, I think she's become an institution in her own right, a presence in the nation and in other realms and territories beyond these shores. At once indomitable, somehow timeless, able to span the generations. Wise, loving, with an utterly irresistible mischievousness of spirit. A mostly strong character, combined with a unique, natural grace and an infectious optimism about life itself.

Above all, though, she understood the British character, and her heart belonged to this ancient old land and its equally indomitable and humorous inhabitants whom she served with panache, style and unswerving dignity for very nearly 80 years.

I know too what she meant to the whole of my family, particularly to the Queen, for whom she was always such a stalwart and sensitive support ever since my grandfather died when he was only two-and-a-half years older than I am now.

And for me, she meant everything, and I had dreaded, dreaded this moment along with, I know, countless others. Somehow, I never thought it would come. She seemed gloriously unstoppable and ever since I was a child, I adored her. Her houses were always filled with an atmosphere of fun, laughter and affection, and I learned so much from her of immense value in my life. Apart from anything else, she wrote such sparklingly wonderful letters, and her turn of phrase could be utterly memorable.

But, above all, she saw the funny side of life, and we laughed 'til we cried, and oh how I shall miss those laughs. And the wonderful wisdom borne of so much experience and of an innate sensitivity to life. She was, quite simply, the most magical grandmother you could possibly have, and I was utterly devoted to her. Her departure has left an irreplaceable chasm in countless lives that, thank God, we're all richer for the sheer joy of her presence and everything she stood for.'

HRH The Prince of Wales
1 April 2002

92

Index

Abdication 49-50, 51
Airlie, Lady 26, 27, 28
Alah 9, 14, 17, 37, 39
Archbishop of Canterbury 32, 50, 53, 79
Archbishop of York 32
Armstrong-Jones, Lady Sarah 5
Asquith, Lady 20
Astor, Lady 46
Australia 39, 40, 69

Baldwin, Stanley 49
Balmoral 61, 62, 80
'Benjamins' 9, 10, 11, 12, 14, 17, 19
Bobs 10, 73
Bowes, George 7
Bowes, Mary Eleanor 7
Bowes-Lyon family 6-7
  Alexander 8, 18, 23; Captain John Patrick 59;
  Cecilia 32, 33; David 9, 10, 13, 14, 17, 18, 19, 23,
  54; Fergus 8, 20, 22, 23; John 8, 20; Mary (Lady
  Elphinstone) 8, 9, 18, 32; Michael 8, 9, 18, 23;
  Patrick 8, 17, 20, 32; Rose 8, 9, 14, 20, 22;
  Violet 8
Bowes- Lyon, Elizabeth (see also Duchess of York
  and Queen Elizabeth) 6-23, 6, 7, 10, 12, 15, 16,
  19, 23, 24, 25, 26, 27, 28, 29, 30, 31, 32
Broadlands 61
Bruton Street 27, 31, 32, 37
Buckingham Palace 13, 26, 31, 32, 40, 54, 56,
  59, 61, 63, 66, 68, 70, 79, 80, 83

Cambridge, Lady May 28, 32, 33
Canada 55
Caribbean 84
Castle of Mey 13, 69
Cator, Elizabeth (Betty) 18, 32, 33
Cavendish- Bentinck family 7
Cazalet, Major Peter 73
Chamberlain, Neville 55
Churchill, Winston 79
Clarence House 26, 66, 70, 72, 73, 84
Coronation 18, 50, 52, 53, 54, 66, 68, 70
Cortachy Castle 27, 28
Court Circular 30
Cozens-Hardy, Mr. 30

Crawford, Miss ('Crawfie') 41
Cunard, Lady 46

Duchess of Kent 43
Duchess of Windsor 50, 51, 56
Duchess of York 32-43, 33, 34, 35, 38, 40, 41, 43,
  44, 46, 47, 48, 49, 54
Duke and Duchess of Teck 34
Duke of Edinburgh 65, 66, 70
Duke of Kent 43, 49, 59
Duke of Windsor 51, 56
Duke of York (see also King George VI) 27, 28, 30,
  32, 33, 34, 35, 36, 37, 38, 39, 40, 41,
  42, 43, 47, 49

East Africa 65
Edinburgh 49, 54
Elphinstone, Elizabeth 18, 32, 33

Farquhar, Lord and Lady 26, 27
Ferguson, Sarah 74, 77, 80
Fort Belvedere 46, 47
France 54
Frogmore House 34
Furness, Lady 46

Germany 56
Glamis Castle 7, 10, 11, 13, 14, 20, 22, 23, 27, 28,
  34, 40, 41
Glamis, Claude Lord (see also Strathmore, Lady) 6,
  7, 8, 9
Greville, Mrs. Ronald 34

Hamilton, Lady Katherine 32, 33
Handley-Seymour 31
Hardinge, Diamond 28, 32, 33
Hartnell, Norman 54
Home Secretary 37, 39, 41

Industrial Welfare Society 35

Joynson-Hicks, Sir William 37

Kensington Palace 80
King Edward VIII 44, 46, 47, 49, 50
King George V 18, 27, 28, 30, 32, 35, 36, 39, 40,
  41, 42, 44, 46, 50
King George VI 45, 50, 52, 53, 54, 55, 56, 58, 59,
  60, 61, 62, 64, 65, 66, 69, 70, 79
King Haakon 56

King James II 37
King Olaf of Norway 21
King Peter 36
Kuebler, Kathie 18, 19

Lacelles, Lord 28
Lang, Mademoiselle (Madé) 14, 18
Leicester, Lady 26
Little House 45, 71
Logue, Lionel 36, 53
Lyon Family 6-7, 13, 23

Mildmay, Lord 73
Mountbatten, Philip (see also the Duke of
  Edinburgh) 61

New Zealand 39, 40
Northern Ireland 37, 54

145 Piccadilly 40, 41, 49
Osborne, Lady Dorothy 17

Polesden Lacey 34
Prince Albert (Prince Consort) 26
Prince Albert (see also Duke of York and King
  George VI) 19, 25, 26, 27, 28
Prince Andrew 71, 74, 81, 82, 89
Prince Charles, Prince of Wales 62, 64, 71, 73, 74,
  75, 77, 79, 80, 89, 90
Prince Edward 81, 83
Prince Harry 80
Prince Henry 32
Prince of Wales (see also King Edward VIII and
  Duke of Windsor) 32, 39, 40, 44, 46
Prince Paul 36
Prince William 80
Princess Anne 64, 71
Princess Christian 35
Princess Elizabeth (see also Queen Elizabeth II) 9,
  38, 39, 43, 49, 53, 59, 60, 61, 63, 65, 73
Princess Margaret 9, 13, 41, 43, 53, 59, 61,
  62, 65, 66, 70, 71, 74
Princess Marina 49
Princess Mary 24, 26, 27, 28, 39
Princess of Wales 21, 75
Princess Olga 36

Queen Elizabeth (Consort and The Queen
  Mother) 10, 13, 16, 20, 21, 26, 37, 45, 50-79, 51,
  52, 54, 56, 57, 58, 59, 60, 61, 63, 64, 65, 67,
  68, 69, 71, 72, 73, 74

Queen Elizabeth II 16, 59, 65, 66, 69, 70, 71,
  77, 83, 89
Queen Marie of Romania 36
Queen Mary 18, 26, 28, 29, 30, 32, 34, 39, 40, 41,
  42, 46, 47, 50, 51, 52, 53, 65, 69, 70
Queen Mary of Modena 37
Queen Victoria 26-7, 35
Queen Wilhelmina 56

Royal Lodge 41, 71, 84
Rhys-Jones, Sophie 81, 83
Sandringham 30, 37, 41, 42, 50, 65, 84
Scotland 34, 41, 49, 54, 69
Scottish Women's Hospital 35
Simpson, Ernest 46
Simpson, Mrs. Wallis (see also Duchess of Windsor)
  46, 47, 49, 50
Simpson, Sir Henry 37
Snowdon, Lord 72
South Africa 13, 61
Southern Rhodesia 71
Spencer, Earl Winfield 46
Spencer, Lady Diana 73, 74, 77, 80, 83, 90
St. James' Square 10, 11, 27
St. Paul's Walden Bury 6, 7, 8, 9, 10, 23, 26, 28,
  30, 41
Star, The 30
Strathmore, Earl of 7, 11, 18, 20, 24, 27, 30, 59
Strathmore, Lady 10, 12, 13, 14, 17, 18, 19, 20,
  22, 23, 24, 28, 30, 37, 54, 55
Streatham Castle 11

Thynne, Lady Mary 28, 32, 33
Townsend, Group Captain Peter 70, 71, 72

United States 55, 70
University of London 72, 73

VE Day 59, 79

Wales 54
Warden of the Cinque Ports 73
Westminster Abbey 28, 31, 32, 53, 70
White Lodge 34, 36, 37
Windsor 45
Windsor Castle 13, 83
World War I 19-23, 24, 27
World War II 55, 56-9, 61, 79